FIND YOUR
Mini
Pumpkin

LIFE LESSONS *to live* WITH PURPOSE

GRENDEL'S
LOFT
PUBLISHING

grendelsloftpublishing@gmail.com

ISBN: 979-8-9866470-0-5 (paperback)
ISBN: 979-8-9866470-1-2 (ebook)

Ordering Information:
Special discounts are available on quantity purchases by corporations, associations, and others. For details, contact grendelsloftpublishing@gmail.com or visit https://author-victoriashort.com.

FIND YOUR
Mini
Pumpkin

LIFE LESSONS *to live* WITH PURPOSE

Victoria Short

Find Your Mini Pumpkin: Life Lessons to Live with Purpose

A book of essays for graduating seniors and adults who wonder what life can be as we wander its path.

About the Author

Victoria Short worked as an English teacher for 28 years, starting her career through the Teach for America program. She holds a B.A. in English from Lafayette College and an M.A. in education from Harvard University. Short served as a lieutenant in the U.S. Army as a military intelligence officer.

She currently resides in Bucks County, Pennsylvania.

Dedication

This book is lovingly dedicated to all of my students, who continue to inspire me. And especially to Bekah Goodwin and Deanna Mikalauskas, who kept records and the faith.

Contents

Our Expression

To the Authentic Self Be True

Living Gracefully

Serendipitous Stuff

The Curveballs in Life

Managing the Hard Stuff

Being Present to Receive

Foreword

4/24/2021 10:57 am From: Hannah   To: Victoria

Our Hannah has just
purchased a pair of Leah
McSweeney high
waisted light wash mom
jeans ...

Idk how I feel about
them, but I decided to
seize the moment. I
blame your chapter on
seizing the moment.

It was actually the
chapter on travel. But it
had a very "go where the
wind blows you" vibe.
And it was breezy today.
And it blew me towards
mom jeans.

Upon meeting Victoria Short during a department meeting one day, it quickly became apparent to me that she was one of The Others. What is an Other, you ask? Others are those people you meet who seem to fly a little higher than the rest, not in self-righteous attitude but in pure spirit. Those people who are innately good at a job, who offer the best counsel, who cause you to cry in front of them but not in a bad way, who challenge everyone they meet to be the best version of themselves. I'm not going to lie—Others made me nervous.

Fast forward approximately six years (my camera folder was wiped out, but the downloads folder is intact and the Norman Reedus memes date back that far) and I'm proud to count The Other as one of my closest friends. What seemed like a solely bookish exterior was quickly peeled away to reveal a delightful array of other veneers. There's the layer that live texts The Real Housewives of New York with me every Wednesday night. There's the layer that accompanied me to a Walking Dead convention wearing matching shirts that read "Don't Open Dead Inside." There's the layer that helped develop the hashtag #broadchurched for when one is blinded by distrust for everyone in sight. The layer that once spent a week planning an actual heist as part of a challenge I sent her. The layer that dyed her signature blonde hair brown because I dared her to. The layer that once filmed a ridiculous video diary for me and then accidentally emailed it to a total stranger. The layer that got downright giddy over receiving a bowie knife as a birthday gift.

If you're starting to think we may not be the best influence on each other I would understand your concern (I'm honestly still not sure why I bought her a knife). But there is also the layer that took a stand against the expectations placed upon teachers. The layer that encouraged her friends to pursue their passion projects. The layer that inspired thousands of students. The layer that can boast about interviewing Snoop Dogg on the red carpet. The layer that taught Life Lessons every Friday, which her students begged to have turned into a book which you now hold. The layer that might loathe being described as an Other but is the most Other of The Others I've ever met.

I'd like to commit an atrocious English teacher sin and state that, in conclusion, I leave you with a necessary bastardization of these lyrics from The Kinks:

Victoria is our queen.

Long may she reign!

—*Hannah*

Introduction

They say there are 36 dramatic situations in the literary tradition. I maintain they can be boiled down to one theme: the search for identity. With that premise, I hoped to invite my students to recognize themselves or people they knew in classic novels we read in class.

The life lesson I presented to them would, I hoped, help connect them to literature that had been written as long as 400 years ago in a world so different from their own that it might as well have taken place on Mars.

It all started with Curley from *Of Mice and Men*. The boss's son, beset by insecurity, is humiliated by every ranch hand in descending order of respect. Curley's only hope of saving face is to attack the biggest guy in the room, the gentle Lennie, who dreams only of rabbits. Curley starts pummeling Lennie without mercy. Only with George's encouragement to "Get 'im, Lennie," are the tables turned and Curley gets his hand crushed beyond recognition. In my life lesson, this scene segues to the story of the scar on my father's thumb, earned from breaking up a bar fight between his friend Joey, short in stature and easily provoked, and a much bigger guy.

Over time, my "Friday Life Lessons" began to focus on daily living and took on a life beyond the literature. They were tied to the premise that high school classes do not address many experiences we will undoubtedly encounter on the road ahead.

The lessons resonated with my students and also with their parents. The topics would resurface at the dinner table and spark connections outside of the classroom too. Literature presents conflicts where people rise, fall, or perhaps just broker an uneasy peace. Daily living similarly challenges us, whether the obstacles are minor inconveniences or defining moments.

There are specific rites of passage where young adults leave the safety of their childhood homes and strike out on their own. Graduation is the most obvious of these. However, throughout life, we are all confronted with opportunities to learn and to grow. The goal of this book is to offer opportunities to pause and to reflect when faced with life's vicissitudes. It's not a guidebook so much as an invitation to be mindful in our choices, reactions, and principles.

Preface

Although this book is full of advice, I offer it with a caveat. We are all individuals with our own paths to travel. In fact, I was once described by a dear friend as "an other," to which other dear friends readily agreed. I have never been married and have no children. Your journey will not look like mine. My intention is to support a practice of mindfulness in the choices you do make.

My life has taken a roundabout way to meaningful purpose, and as always self-doubt is along for the journey. My hope is that my words about this earthly experience will make you more thoughtful about your own choices. If showing up is half the battle, being mindful is undoubtedly the other half. As I used to tell my students during my 28-year teaching career, you need not agree with me. In fact, if you disagree with me, it is only an indication that you're confident in your own staunch character. And that's a good thing.

LIVING LIFE

The Gift of Gratitude

The old adage states that grateful people are happier people. But gratitude is best served by specificity. Of course, you are grateful for your health, friends, and family. But you don't want your daily affirmations to sound like generic platitudes.

Every fall during my teaching career, I would pick up a mini pumpkin from a local grocery store. Technically, they are gourds, but to me, they will always be mini pumpkins. Wearing a silly grin, I would hold up this treasure to my students. For color, shape, and size, there are few things more beautiful. "Look at the symmetry," I would marvel. "Note the portability," I would state as I raised and lowered the gourd with two fingers.

My message? I am not, by nature, wildly optimistic. Yet, when the autumn arrives and I hold that mini pumpkin in the palm of my hand, I cannot help but revel in the fact that I live in a world capable of such splendor. It's hard to stay sad, mad, frustrated, or regretful in that moment.

Everyone needs to find his or her own mini pumpkin. It can be an object, a person, or an idea. It serves as a talisman of wonder and a representation of all that is wonderful, and it is best chosen by the individual.

Over the years, students have given me pumpkins made of yarn and porcelain. Some tell me that they have even bought the little pumpkins for their college dorm rooms. Many more have chosen their own token or concept to hold dear.

Find your mini pumpkin.

An Oatmeal a Day

Conventional wisdom suggests that one must rise in the morning and make the bed. This custom can establish a sense of accomplishment and provide an organizational boost. While not exactly the same, a similar principle can be applied to your nutritional well-being.

Consider getting in the daily habit of eating oatmeal for breakfast. Not the prepackaged, instant kind—I'm talking about rolled oats that aren't sold as individual servings. Consider it an investment in your health. It's also one of those satisfying routines that requires a number of steps and can be a way to nurture the need to start the day off on the right foot with a soothing ritual.

This will allow you to begin the day with a good habit instead of a bad one. An energy drink and a bag of Takis at seven a.m. is what many of my students ate for breakfast. A poor choice in the morning will make it easier to usher in more bad habits to haunt the rest of your day.

If this sounds boring, keep in mind you can embellish your oatmeal with wild abandon. Some suggestions are a banana for extra creaminess, berries for tartness, or perhaps some shaved coconut for texture and flavor. Be liberal with the spices, too. Cinnamon is a must, but why not a dollop of maple syrup or a dash of vanilla extract? (And if the season and mood permit, get creative with nutmeg and pumpkin spice.) In addition to the heart health benefits, this is a meal that keeps you full and energized for hours. Bottom line, if you haven't the time or means for oatmeal, it's time to reevaluate your life.

Daily Personal Maintenance

1. *Forgive yourself.* It develops your compassion. We've all done things that make us cringe upon reflection. My teacher friends used to call it 'perseverating.' Perhaps you relive the event with new variables, saying or doing the things in your imagination you wish you'd done in real life. It's time to let it go and try to do better next time. By giving yourself a break, you may also be more likely to do the same for others who are harder to forgive.

2. *Breathe deeply.* It grounds the soul. Few of us actually breathe properly. We're either taking shallow breaths or hyperventilating. One of the benefits of mediation is the concentration it promotes on the breath. I'm not sure I knew what my diaphragm even was before I started to practice mindful breathing. Now whenever I'm in a stressful situation, the

first thing I do is become aware of my breath rather than racing back into the breach. Give yourself time to become calm and measured. What proceeds from that state will always be reasonable and inspired.

3. *Accept compliments.* It promotes grace. In other words, don't be so quick to retort when someone makes a flattering remark about you. Don't ruin the moment by trying to insert modesty where a little celebration is in order.

Life Hacks for the Night Before

If you aren't a morning person, here are some things to consider doing the night before a workday:

→ Write down anything that is concerning you about the day to come. It might be school, the office, or the in-laws. Then include one proactive step you can take in the morning to address the concern. It might be an email, a phone call, or a conversation. In doing so, you give such cares the time they deserve. (This is particularly important on Sunday evenings.) Although it's easier said than done, it's important not to drag apprehensions to bed.

→ Frame tomorrow and its possibilities in a positive light. A friend of mine suggests that we ought to describe our plans as "I get to" rather than "I have to." *I get to scrub the toilet* may seem to stretch this practice to its limits, but it does characterize the task as a chance at improvement rather than as an unenviable chore. Short of confronting what is, however, you have the capacity and indeed the responsibility to reimagine your circumstances in ways that are uplifting and empowering.

Know the Exits, Find the Bathrooms

It's a good idea to be aware of your surroundings. Whenever I go into a building, I like to know how to get back out. In a hurry if need be. And I also want to know where to *go*, if you know what I mean.

When I was a substitute teacher, the same rule applied and was of particular importance because I could be sent to a different campus in the district on any given day. In schools, one also wants to make the acquaintance of those who are truly in charge of the building—namely the secretaries and the custodians. They make up the first line of defense.

In other words, know the lay of the land in a structured environment. Whether it's a café, a subway, a stadium, or an airplane, have a plan of escape and know where the bathroom is. (Oh, and when the flight attendant is making his or her presentation, give your full attention.)

Don't wait for the crisis to realize you don't have a plan of action.

The Commute

For a time, I commuted from Pennsylvania to Hoboken, New Jersey. It was a daily trip fraught with horror.

Everyone around me on the highway looked grim and slightly crazed. No one seemed to like the idea of where they were going, but they were certainly attempting to get there first. I've been told by my British relatives that American drivers are far more courteous than European ones. I'm inclined to believe that. This does not, however, extend to rush hour.

I would often recognize the same people on the road and almost wanted to wave. I did not. They were angry people and rather intimidating. I'm not an aggressive driver and will happily defer to the whims of others on the highway. The true test of wills came with the Pulaski Skyway. It sounds enchanting, like a ride at Disney. It's anything but magical. It requires one to merge with the pack of stampeding water buffalo in about six feet.

Once I reached Hoboken, I had to begin the search for parking. At the time I taught at Hoboken Charter School, which was housed within another school facility. There was no parking available for teachers outside the host school, so we had to fend for ourselves. This is why people who own cars in major cities often boast about the on-street parking they have secured.

Driving requires a person's full attention to stay safe and is not the time for multitasking. For this reason, it's best to get off your phone. This is also not the time to extend your office hours.

Instead, commuting offers time for an investment in *you*. Use this part of your day to dream beyond your current state about what's possible while you keep your eyes on the road and your mind off potential annoyances.

The Money Pie

The experts suggest we spend no more than 30% of our income on housing.[1] Good luck with that. However, if the cost of housing is eclipsing everything else, it's time to reevaluate. Even a job you love is going to feel like nothing more than a hamster wheel if you're struggling to break even each month.

Track your bills, checkbook entries, credit card statements, and cash expenditures to know exactly where you stand. Knowledge is power, and ignorance is expensive.

Children don't need to be sheltered from financial realities. Yes, they should feel secure. They should not, however, be subjected to deception in an attempt to keep up appearances. They are far savvier than we realize.

Education is a fine investment, but if you're going to risk your own retirement by funding your child's college tuition,

1   Rebecca Lake, "Rule of Thumb: How Much Should You Spend on Rent?" The Balance, updated October 30, 2021, https://www.thebalance.com/what-percentage-of-your-income-should-go-to-rent-4688840.

you're committing a disservice to both you and your child. There are loans, grants, scholarships, and other choices available. I used to urge parents to access all of the resources available through the guidance department, the college, and the career center in high school. I always got the feeling there was money left on the table because people were not informed about all the possible funding opportunities.

The best approach is to instill in your child a healthy respect for money, including how it is earned and how it can be allocated for the best return on investment.

Pay Yourself First

This is common and quite solid advice. It simply means investing in oneself. The goal is to invest 10% of your earnings for the long haul. The percentage, however, is less important than the commitment itself. If you can make the contribution automatically through direct deposit, then you're less likely to miss it. Investigate opportunities to invest in a 401(k) or a 403(b) if such options are offered by your company. If you work for yourself, the same goal still applies.

If you believe managing finances and investments is outside your wheelhouse, you can employ the services of a financial advisor who can help you to build a portfolio and manage risk. The key is to be mindful without being preoccupied with your investments. The market will ebb and flow. If you're sufficiently diversified in those investments, you can weather the storm. With regular contributions, your nest egg will grow.

The goal of wealth is freedom and security. This will allow

you to pursue your dreams without financial obstacles and provide safety and opportunity for your family. Investing in yourself helps to accomplish these goals. If you want to build generational wealth, this is the path.

The Latte Factor

My signature drink at Starbucks was a grande soy no foam latte. It was a luxury, but as I reasoned, a modest one.

I am no coffee snob. I'll drink coffee from Wawa, Dunkin' Donuts, or whatever I have available at home. But there's something about Starbucks. Perhaps it's because they have baristas, or because you get to order in fake Italian, or because successful people look natural holding the product.

I would routinely stop there for my daily latte after school as a wee reward for making it through another day. That cost me four dollars a pop and $20 a week. Imagine investing that money over 20 years. Yes, it makes me wince too.

Years ago, I invested in a $14 coffeepot from CVS that has lasted far longer than I could have hoped. It is an integral part of my morning routine. Making my own coffee is no mindless habit born of sheer repetition. I choose salted caramel when I'm feeling light-hearted and Sumatra when I'm hoping for a sharper focus. I have a mug that is the perfect size for coffee as opposed to the cups I reserve for tea. The point is this morning ritual is easier, more enjoyable, and definitely more cost-efficient than my former practice.

Bottom line: If you can afford it, treat yourself to your heart's content. However, if you are wondering where all the money goes, identify your own latte factor, and pamper yourself in a more fiscally responsible, if no less decadent, way.

Everyone Needs
a Mentor

I have several mentors. Some of them are older, and some of them are younger. Everyone has his or her preference, and selfishly or not, I like to hear the hard-won wisdom of others. You don't need to hang on every word proffered by another, but the concept I return to often is perspective, and that is the greatest gift a mentor can provide.

The arrangement can be formal or informal. The goal is to learn information that's worth knowing from someone with the wisdom and time to teach.

In this same vein, it's also important to *be* a mentor. If you have children or younger siblings, guess what—you probably already are one. There's an inherent responsibility in knowing this fact. You don't actually have to say a word either. The way you conduct your life becomes the living example.

Everyone Needs a Project

This advice is actually from my Uncle Michael. He was a very talented chef, briefly a model, and by the end, a hopeless alcoholic. He had a charisma that women found intoxicating and a nasty edge—both delivered with an English accent.

We didn't see eye to eye often, but I appreciated his talent. His restaurants were always successful, and he'd run them until he grew bored and longed for a new adventure. When he did, he'd sell the business for a song to an eager protégé and move on.

My friend Susan once heard him say that "Everyone needs a project," and the advice has stuck with both of us. It keeps life fun and intriguing, just in case work itself isn't a source of inspiration. I think that's why Michael frequently sold his restaurants to start a new one. An established successful business was rewarding but not necessarily stimulating. He had a knack for knowing when to move on and when to begin again.

Put another way, we all need something to be excited about that we can create. We may find it with our families, in our work, or through service to others. If you haven't found a project that inspires you, seek it out and nurture it.

Minimalism

Not everything I own brings me joy. One example might be cat litter (though it could be argued that my quality of life would suffer without it). Minimalism, a trendy way of decluttering, operates for me on both a literal and metaphorical level. Clutter, whether literal or existential, robs us of so much energy. When you clear out *the stuff*, the emotional burden can often lift.

Minimalism is not for everyone. If you're comforted by plenty, then embrace it. Essentialism does not necessarily mean spartan. Possessions are to be appreciated, perhaps even cherished.

But our stuff should neither inconvenience nor overwhelm. If the need to protect possessions is overshadowing the pleasure of having them, it's time to take stock. If they become more important than loved ones, that's a problem.

Be mindful if you find yourself paying for storage while you're moving or waiting for a space that can house your possessions. Much like interest on a credit card, you're simply paying for your things over and over again. Ask yourself if it's worth it.

The practice of paring down and retaining favorites works well in my cozy loft apartment. It makes tidying up and finding items quickly much easier. I enjoy honoring what I own and making mindful choices about what comes into my personal space.

If you wish to experiment with minimalism, start small. Set a goal of reducing the superfluous. This may be an individual pursuit or a family affair. Remember that you can sell, donate, or recycle. Broken or expired items should be thrown away. Whether or not you pursue Marie Kondo or feng shui levels of commitment and minimalism, like many things, it will operate on a continuum.

Broken Doesn't Heal Itself

I used to have individual whiteboards for my students. Initially, the plan was to use them to check for understanding among my freshmen. It turns out that my seniors also enjoyed an impromptu whiteboard review. I handed out colorful markers too. The instruction was that if the marker wore out, they should throw it away. But more often than not, students chucked the dead markers back in the box. What was the thinking here? Did they expect the markers to regenerate themselves?

How often do we do the same in our own lives? Don't put the broken items back—they won't recover. Either mend them or pitch them. In other words, address the situation. This is not about assigning blame. Why did my students want to cover the fact that the marker ran out? That's what markers do.

Some things resolve themselves over time. That's *not* what

we're discussing here. If you are making excuses or ignoring something that needs to be addressed, don't procrastinate. Just get it done.

Guilty Pleasures

When it comes to guilty pleasures, I'm neither proud nor repentant. Mine include watching episodes of *Real Housewives*, searching for YouTube videos on tiny house living, and indulging on Hershey's Kisses. I could go on, but there's no good reason to expose every secret.

One of my greatest guilty pleasures is napping, because it feels like wasted time. I'd like to believe I have a healthy work ethic, and I take pride in being productive and feeling accomplished. Napping feels indulgent and decadent. But oddly, as I get older, I've learned to make my peace with napping. I love napping in the sun. Sometimes it can be an escape, but normally it's restorative.

As my friend Susan says, "Everybody knows the score." I'm not big on sports analogies, but this one resonates. In other words, we know our own truths. If you need a break, then take a break. If you want to nap in the sun like a cat, then do so. Embrace the full human experience. There's a time for it all.

Get Your House in Order

My aunt and cousin passed away in close succession. I was the executor. The paperwork they'd left helped me to navigate the probate process with clarity. It still took 18 months to settle and had its share of unforeseen moving parts. There were vehicles, property, and accounts to address—not to mention 17 electric guitars. But the end-of-life wishes had been clearly articulated. It made all the difference, and I was able to easily follow the intentions of my family members. I felt honored, humbled, and grateful.

We don't like to think about the end of our time here but denying the inevitable doesn't make it go away. Let me speak plainly: you need a will and a power of attorney and an advanced health directive. Make sure they are legally binding. Do it soon. If you have children or other dependents, do it now.

THROUGH THE LENS

Perspective

Do you secretly catastrophize?

When I think of all the time I've wasted worrying about what wasn't even a problem, it's sobering indeed. In truth, it's generally not as bad as you think it's going to be. If you decide *not* to do something, let it be because it will put someone in grave danger, not because of your fragile feelings, your stage fright, or your irrational fear of the dentist. Yes, that last one is all mine.

You cannot monetize worrying. In other words, there's no return on the investment. You cannot impress others with the depth of your anguish. The time that you fritter away imagining the worst is far better spent invested in the mission itself. Remember, we're not talking about the welfare of your children. We're discussing the relatively trivial tasks that will crowd a typical day. If you've done all you can do and have considered the time and resources at your disposal, then your obligation has been met.

Remember, you have no sway over the opinions of others. Recognizing what lies outside of your control can be a great help in mitigating worry.

Many of my fellow teachers would stress when an administrator observed their class. Naturally an educator wants to demonstrate her skill and protect her job security. But the years of training, the daily practice of teaching, and the rapport built with students are at work during that observed lesson. So, the investment in success has already been made.

If your worry stems from the knowledge that you're woefully unprepared or overwhelmed, then address those concerns. Advocate for yourself by asking for more time or more training. If the moment is at hand and there's simply no means of further preparation, then all that is left to do is your best.

Trust Your Gut

We all have a sixth sense. The message may come from within, above, or beyond, whatever you want to believe (I'm not sure myself). What I do know is that intuition is real. We've all experienced walking into a room and feeling a palpable tension. We perceive something in a way that may not be available to our traditional five senses. I'm a firm believer in trusting this intuition—it's the voice of our more conscious selves.

If that means leaving a situation without explanation, then that's what you must do. Don't worry about being embarrassed. You can apologize or explain yourself later.

When my mother first came to this country, she was still in high school, and she enjoyed driving around the neighborhood in her first car. On one of those trips, she drove down a street where several homeowners had gathered around a tree that was leaning ominously over the street. It had been struck by lightning the day before. A man was in the street stopping cars as they approached and convinced each driver to turn around. When my mother drove up, she received the same warning. In typical teenager fashion, she pointed out that if he hadn't stopped her, she would already be on the other side of the tree. The man backed up to let her pass.

As she tells the story, she had every intention of driving forward. Yet, as she went to step on the gas, there was an unmistakable voice in her head. It was a male voice, and it sternly said, "*Turn around!*" She did so. And the tree came down.

I can say with conviction that I'm very grateful my mother listened to that voice.

Intrinsic Motivation

I was a Girl Scout in the '70s. There was only one badge I actually earned: the writer's badge. My friend Lisa convinced her mother to host a writing workshop with half a dozen of us. I distinctly remember a bohemian-style living room with ample snacks. Somehow, Lisa's mother was able to assume the role of host, coach, and cheerleader. Inspired by her hospitality and wit, we produced a one-act play. I felt so accomplished, even at that tender age. And I really treasured that badge.

Our Girl Scout leader was a hard-edged woman who chain-smoked. At one of our meetings, she pulled out a manual and began listing badges she thought we had earned. I think we all knew that she was feeling inadequate to the task and just wanted to order a bunch of badges. (Most of them had to do with nature. To my recollection, we never left the rec room in our leader's house.) That was the day I learned about intrinsic motivation, although it would be years before I could call it that.

Those badges were a farce and hollow, and I just couldn't bring myself to sew them onto my sash. Worthless accolades fool no one and impress no one, at least not over time. But that writer's badge. *That* was special.

Seize the Morning

Thoughts are powerful things that help to shape and define our reality.

Much of what we think comes from a short list of habitual thoughts. It's sobering that we are driven largely by a level of pre-thought that is, more often than not, negative.

I'm forever grateful for my opportunity to be a high school English teacher. However, I can say with equal conviction that when the alarm went off at 4:15 a.m., my waking thought was one of annoyance and dread. Once I got where I was going, I was fine, but leaving the bed and facing the commute? That was another matter. For better or worse, that feeling of resistance became hard-wired. I never greeted the day. I acquiesced to it. In retrospect, I wonder about the missed chances of those mornings. I can only guess what could have been possible if I had treasured those waking moments as opportunities for inspiration and reflection.

The Memory of the Azalea Bushes

My earliest memory is standing in my backyard on Long Island, on the border of the Schmidts' yard, and marveling at the azalea bushes. Wait, it gets better. I said to myself, *It's important to remember this day and these flowers because life goes by so fast.* I must have been about five. It would be at least another 30 years before I had a notion that could rival it.

Children are capable of such stunning insights. Never assume that they're not listening to us and shaping themselves into who they will become.

Emotional Intelligence

Apparently, I'm emotionally stunted. I know this because I learned through my studies that to be fully evolved, one should both empathize with others and control one's own emotions. And it does make sense. If there's a humanitarian crisis afoot, tears and handwringing will do little to address the problem. A level head and a logical mind are what is needed.

But I'll just have to settle for arrested development. If you start crying, I'll start crying. Unfortunately, I sometimes made students cry. I assure you, it was never my intent. It always happened when I was trying to offer students compassionate counsel on how to rise to the occasion and set things right.

I'm not going to tell you how to raise your kids. You have my full respect for taking on the role of parent. It's a part I'll never play. But I've been blessed to have many young people in my life who are filled with hormones, humor, and humanity. The best and worst thing about kids is their candor. You always know where you stand with a group of teenagers. The only advice I'll give is this: Don't try to be one of them. Kids are not looking for our friendship. What they need is our guidance and understanding. Rather than simply empathizing with students, our role as a teacher, mentor, or parent should be to offer guidance—dispassionately. Our empathy supports the instinct to get involved. Our foresight can help us provide what kids need.

Consider the Source

We've all received criticism, and that's not a bad thing. That being said, there's the constructive type and the simply insulting variety. Be aware of the situation, the speaker's motivation, and the potential positive returns.

If the advice is unsolicited, don't reject it out of hand. If we don't realize there's a problem to begin with, we're unlikely to seek solutions. An outside view can bring a refreshing objectivity. The problem arises when someone is diminishing our contributions or confidence because they're seeking to enhance their own.

Consider the advice that begins with, "Well, I wouldn't do it" and ends with "but you do you" to be of questionable value.

If you actively seek out someone's opinion, either let it be a person whom you trust and has your best interests at heart or an industry expert who can be unbiased.

Also consider your own expectations. Are you willing to hear a harsh truth? Will you tie the fate of a friendship, a mentorship, or a working relationship to a positive review? Are you truly seeking advice or an endorsement of your own decision?

If there's something to be gained from uncomfortable moments, it's worth knowing. If the offering is mean-spirited, it's perfectly acceptable to reject such comments. One of the many blessings that comes with age is a clearer discernment about what matters and what we can grow from.

In the Land of Boudreaux and Thibodaux Jokes

I love regionalisms. I spent seven years teaching in south Louisiana and experienced a delightful dose of culture shock.

The French, Spanish, and African influences, combined with the echoes of the native Chitimacha and Choctaw, create a colorful palette of traditions, distinction, assimilation, and preservation. This helped me discover Kate Chopin, a 19th-century writer who addressed racial discrimination and women's emancipation in ways that were both poignant and poetic.

I visited her home in Cloutierville, which has since burned down in 2008. I traveled to Grand Isle, looking for the grandeur of the 19th-century Creoles in much the same way my father searched for the vanishing Old West of fable in the 1950s. I arrived far too late, as did he. All this I would share with my students in Louisiana and back in Pennsylvania as they shook their heads at the perceived selfishness of Edna Pontellier in Chopin's *The Awakening*. "It's difficult to identify with an unsympathetic protagonist, isn't it?" I would offer. "That's one way to put it," they would say.

Sometimes we need to step outside of what we take for granted to appreciate what has been found—and irretrievably lost. That was one of the many gifts of Louisiana. I used to hang out in Jackson Square in New Orleans on the weekends and imagine the world of Anne Rice. Soon, there came a nod of recognition from the fortune tellers and artists who plied their craft in the square. I was no longer a tourist, but now somewhat of an insider. There was a café I used to frequent that had marvelous architecture and few customers. The tourists, I reasoned, were across the French Quarter at Café Du Monde with their beignets. Here I would get the real story.

In actuality, the real story was in my classroom, where my students prepared me for Hurricane Andrew. Up until then, I thought hurricanes were just thunderstorms with names. This is also where I would learn that students would include my own phrasing in their essays. I had to stop informally referring to Estella in *Great Expectations* as "creepy girl." The most touching was a seventh grader who had written "in the soul of the bale," in an attempt to say *inconsolable*. His version was somehow more poignant.

Of course, every region contains regionalisms. We just take the ones in our own neighborhood for granted.

Americans Abroad

I'm routinely mistaken for being Canadian when I travel. When I finally asked why, you might guess the bashful answer that was given. Let's face it. Americans have a reputation for being rude, brash, demanding, and entitled when we travel. It's a stereotype, nothing more. However, in such cases, there's often a grain of truth, right? And here's what I've come to believe. It's not that Americans are overbearing. We simply are not fully committed to leaving home.

Travel isn't about replicating what you know. The goal is to embrace something new. The sights, the cuisine, the landscape, and most of all, the people. For creatures of comfort, there's always a measure of unease when we're in unfamiliar territory. To achieve a pure experience, you'll need to *get off the bus*. Do not see the destination of your dreams through a smudged window on an organized tour.

It begins with the mindset. By all means, do your research,

but what I am suggesting is that you immerse yourself in the opportunity to explore. Don't arrive with preconceived ideas or be in a rush to compare this experience to what you've known in the past. Simply be a traveler embracing an authentic journey.

You may not be down for the youth hostel experience, but consider avoiding the big resorts that pamper uneasy travelers. Instead, consider smaller hotels, B&Bs, or house sharing opportunities that encourage you to become acquainted with local towns and villages. Seek out occasions for breaking bread with the residents. And, naturally, visit the famous sites, honor the country's sources of national pride, and contribute to their economy.

I was traveling in New Zealand in the early months of 1991 when Operation Desert Storm began. As a result, I saw precious few Americans during my trip, and I appreciated that. I love my people, but I had not traveled thousands of miles to hang out with them. Joining a group of mainly European backpackers, I had the opportunity to attend a dinner at a Maori community. When we arrived, we were informed that the community was still in mourning for a young girl. Our initial reaction was to head back to the van to allow our hosts to grieve in peace. However, we were assured that we were most welcome. It was only that their time of sorrow needed to be acknowledged.

Without quite realizing what was happening, I was chosen by our group as the spokesperson to acknowledge the loss. I don't remember what I said, but while speaking, I saw a Maori woman tear up and I knew I was done for. I cannot watch someone cry without joining in. There were many tears shed that evening and

I have never felt so immediately drawn to strangers in all my life.

When you seek an authentic experience, you might just find a universal one.

Metacognition

Metacognition is a fascinating concept. Thinking about thinking. It's like taking a peek behind the curtain of the stage performance.

One of my roommates in Louisiana introduced me to the notion of our "schema." It's one of those popular educational buzzwords that explains the cognitive framework by which we organize and interpret information. I've always wondered where information goes when we momentarily forget it, but it's not irretrievably lost. I suspect it's floating through our schema looking for a connection to find the way back.

This is why no experiences are ever truly wasted—good or bad, uplifting or painful. We naturally look for ways to weave them into the larger landscape of our lives.

We Inherit the Features and Earn the Face

The gray hair and the wrinkles. Yep, I earned them. In retrospect, I probably should have reached for the sunscreen a few more times, but I'm generally at peace with what I see in the mirror. There's no way to halt the passage of time. If you want to look younger, there's no shame in creams and cosmetic procedures, but I often think we would do better to work on the stuff inside. If you still want to look and feel better, find ways to laugh and smile more. Authentically. If you've got nothing to smile about, change your perspective.

Seeing All Sides

I had the privilege of teaching AP Seminar for a year. The course is designed to teach research skills to students, seeing them through the process of crafting a question, building an argument with evidence, and publishing and presenting to an audience. One of the most valuable aspects of the course is the focus on vetting resources and identifying bias. For example, one might want to question a drug trial sponsored by the pharmaceutical company that stands to profit from the drug's distribution.

In these times of polarized and polarizing political views, it's important to find balanced reporting. In the absence of objective reporting of the news, you might want to listen to opposing biased positions, including those that challenge your own current beliefs, before reaching your own conclusions. Be prepared for the possibility that your position is nuanced. While it is tempting and gratifying to listen to platforms that champion your views rather than challenging them, it is important to resist this urge.

These days, there's a whole lot of grandstanding going on. That's why it's always a good idea to identify the stakeholders for the issue. Politics are often beset with baggage, including constituents, loyalties, favors, and viability.

We will never get anywhere if we're not willing to put ourselves in other people's shoes and consider their points of view. That doesn't mean we will ever understand a contrary position firsthand or demonstrate grace when an opposing view is presented. But it is a step.

Start with examining your own experience. We all have bias. It's not an evil to be overcome. It exists in all races, religions, and communities. I would ask anyone who is attempting to seize the moral high ground to remember that humans tend to be myopic in their world views to varying degrees. You don't have to surrender your position, but you might want to explore how you became invested in it.

Winning Life's Lottery

Okay, not to get too technical, but what are the chances of the sperm and egg that made you meeting? Two people had to come together and do the deed at just the right moment. What are the odds? Infinitesimally small. According to Mel Robbins, the chances are one in 400 trillion.[2] I think about the butterfly effect and how, however subtle the impact, we all have a connection to one another simply through our mere existence. As I used to remind my students, you are here for a reason. Figure out what makes you happy and enjoy the journey for all it is worth.

---

2   Mel Robbins, "How to stop screwing yourself over," TEDxSF, June 2011, https://www.ted.com/talks/mel_robbins_how_to_stop_screwing_yourself_over?language=en.

The Enlightened Self

People are fond of saying that if they could only tell their younger self what they know now, the way might have been less rocky. But there's also wisdom in our current selves speaking to our future selves. I used to have my incoming freshmen write to their graduating selves. Senior year, long after they had forgotten they had even written those letters, they were delivered. I didn't know what they had written, but I loved watching their faces as they read. The most common reaction was a knowing smile.

If you don't want to get other people involved, you can stick the letter in an inconspicuous place on the refrigerator and wait a year or tuck it away and write yourself a note on the calendar. Why not hear insight from an aspirational you? Knowing yourself as well as you do, I'm sure you have an idea of what you want to hear and what you'll *need* to hear.

Record the Laughter of Those You Love

When I was a teenager, I used to tell my friends that dinners were a time of laughter in my house. My parents and I started with the typical questions of how our days had gone, but we always wound up telling stories and laughing. One night, for no particular reason, I captured our dinner conversation with a tape recorder (naturally, for such were the times). I treasure the preservation of that laughter. Pictures are also a great record of the past, but the sound of laughter to evoke special memories is incomparable.

OUR EXPRESSION

The English Language

Do you know the story of how the English language evolved? In the year 1066, William the Conqueror, a Frenchman, invaded what is now England. Rather than one language supplanting another, two languages, Old English and Old French, merged. The combination became the English we know today. But while the languages *merged*, they didn't blend. So, even though the English language has developed over time, the words have retained their distinct origins. (The simple, one-syllable words are Germanic; the fancy ones are French and Latin.) I personally don't find English to be pleasing to the ear. However, one must be impressed by its sheer volume of words. That's why English is rich in nuance and possibility.

We generally get through the day using just a few hundred common words. Consider choosing your words more thoughtfully, especially when the stakes are high. This doesn't mean using big words to impress. It means picking a word that lends precision to your argument. As students develop their own style, some will reach for the thesaurus. This is a helpful tool with which exercising some constraint is prudent. There can be an initial "Mad Libs" period filled with wild experimentation when attempting to make an essay sound more intelligent.

Fun fact: There seems to be a phase many students go through where they glom onto the word "myriad." I remember discovering the word myself as a teenager and sprinkling it in English essays. I'm still wondering what the irresistible appeal of this word is.

Eliminating clutter with regard to language can be equally helpful. There are expressions that have become mere place-holders. The phrase "you know" is buying a speaker time. He's not asking whether his message has been understood. There are other annoying modifiers like "literally" that dilute a message. Things labeled literal rarely are. This adverb is often used to pro-vide emphasis or convey frustration, but there are much better choices that will carry conviction.

The goal is always clarity. Quality language over quantity. Language can be couched, diluted, sanitized, and euphemized. It can also be rendered ambiguous, contradictory, or hollow. We've all heard people use a lot of words to say precious little. At its best, language conveys both the meaning and the spirit of our expression. It shouldn't be used to mask our true intent.[3]

---

3   If you're interested in this topic, I highly recommend you read George Orwell's essay "Politics and the English Language," https://www. orwellfoundation.com/the-orwell-foundation/orwell/essays-and-other-works/politics-and-the-english-language/.

Ditch the Upspeak

Upspeak happens when one ends a statement as if it were a question. I think these speakers are trying to appear upbeat, engaged, and relevant. The people who I have heard use it are generally young, well-intentioned, and invested in how their message is received by others.

I first encountered this annoying trend in college. I figured it was simply a sorority house affectation born of unbridled enthusiasm during rush week. I heard it all year, unfortunately. Problem is, an interrogative statement serves a specific purpose. It is seeking information, not providing it. For this reason, presentations offering information disguised as questions can be unsettling.

When I heard members of school administration do this, I wanted so badly to address it but couldn't figure out a way to not be offensive. If the goal is authenticity in all things, let's be sure to include communication. Declarative and interrogative are two types of sentences with discrete purposes. Let's honor their distinction.

The Handshake

The pandemic has called this time-honored tradition into question, and I hope it returns. If not, I hope a worthy alternative emerges. Bumping elbows simply won't do. A handshake originally demonstrated a promise of peace, to show one was bearing no weapons or thoughts of harm. It has been refined as a movement in the art of the deal.

I addressed this life lesson early in the school year. As with many things, my advice for the handshake was to do it well or not at all. A perfunctory handshake without conviction is distasteful.

A firm handshake with eye contact communicates so much. And there is a sweet spot. Not to be sexist, but among my students, I often saw notable trends. When I asked students to shake hands, girls were often tentative and sometimes nervously giggled. Boys were more adept but often turned the gesture into a challenge. Somewhere in the middle is the goal. Be present and be invested. Stand in your confidence and extend an invitation to collaborate.

Proofread for Grammar—And Then Again for Tone

There's no doubt that if you want an idea to be taken seriously, an error-free proposal has a leg up on the competition. What is less assumed is tone. Tone, whether intended or unintended, conveys at least as much force as the words. Just like avoiding a phone call when angry, it's equally recommended to avoid the written word when upset.

The spelling and syntax may be spot on, but you may be hard-pressed to conceal your emotions. This is why a set of proofreading eyes is prudent. Words carry connotations, nuance, and even double entendre. Unresolved feelings carry sarcasm, condescension, and general smarm for days. Even innocuous phrases carry potential baggage. My students would often start sentences in literary essays with *Anyone can see that...* While I appreciate the confidence, the inherent implication is that if we don't see it, we are fools. If it is that apparent, let the supporting evidence do the convincing.

You're unlikely to begin a communication to your boss with "Dear shit-for-brains..." *But* an otherwise compelling argument can be undone by a single sentence that sticks in the craw of the recipient.

I'm not suggesting that your missives be reduced to politically correct milquetoast. But if a misplaced comma can cause confusion, imagine what a terse attitude can convey. It's in writing and it may be in the cloud. Now, it's a historical artifact. While you can always offer explanations after the fact, do you want to?

If the message is difficult to put into words, consider a conversation instead. When written communication is required, give yourself and its intended reader the time and respect it deserves. If you choose to be strident, rock on. Just remember that thoughtfulness has won more battles.

Hurling Invective

Let's call it what it is: cursing. We all have our personal favorites. However, if I can restrain myself in the classroom, I expect the same from my high school students.

While reading aloud, I was a purist about text—meaning that if it was written, I was going to read it. My students and I had a conversation about this prior to the unit. If anyone felt uncomfortable, they could communicate their concern to me privately, and I'd get more creative with that particular class. I liked to read the word out loud, not because I was looking for a cheap thrill but because I wanted to convey the full impact of what the writer was trying to say.

In literature, curse words must either be in service to characterization or strategically placed for effect. Although there's always the risk of an angered parent, it's important to honor both the book's integrity and the students' maturity. In so doing, there can be a candid conversation that acknowledges the controversy and invites lively debate.

If a student cursed in the heat of the moment and then acknowledged the slip, it was immediately forgiven. Shit happens. But since I was required to stand outside my room between classes to monitor the halls, I did get annoyed at kids dropping the f-bomb nearby. Sure, it's a private conversation, but I'm standing *right here*. If I was in a stall in the girls' bathroom, where there was an expectation of privacy, I'd make my presence known in a joking way, only so I wasn't accused of eavesdropping.

There's an unmistakable allure to cursing. I get it. I'm not a prude. But there is a time and a place. Free expression aside, where is room made for courtesy?

I will say that the F-word is a popular go-to for a reason. It can assume virtually every part of speech. Props must be given for the linguistic versatility. It can be so satisfying in conveying a specific level of frustration, disbelief, and disgust. Sometimes another word simply will not do. But I take offense when it is used ubiquitously, stemming from a lack of imagination.

No matter where you stand on the practice, it is a custom that's built and billed to be in service to one's fellow man. If we can be mandated to protect each other from our breath, can we be mindful, at least, of when and how we feel the need to spew offensive words?

"My Paw-Paw's Got a Nub"

When I started my teaching career in Louisiana, I asked my students to share something from their lives that was unique and only they could tell. One student volunteered: "My Paw-Paw's got a nub."

That sentence has always stayed with me—partly because I'm intrigued by all the names used for grandparents, and partly because I was horrified by the idea of a missing finger. Of course, there was a story behind this declaration, but it can almost stand alone. It is so sure of itself and has so much promise. How did Paw-Paw wind up with a nub? How has he suffered the travail of its aftermath? Why do we get the distinct impression that he's just fine?

I encouraged my students to journal, although I am admittedly not diligent about this practice myself. The trick is to be free from self-consciousness. The raw phrasing is the best and most closely matches the writer's current mood. If one is struggling to journal or far too self-conscious to do so, I highly recommend creating ragged haikus. This is not about format so much as capturing a moment in time. The practice is also an excellent creative writing activity and a way to provide inspiration for the college essay.

Public and Permanent

If a child is old enough to have access to a computer or a smartphone, he or she should also know about the notion of "public and permanent"—that whatever digital content is posted is an artifact in perpetuity. Sadly, in our rush to make technology available to the upcoming generations, we have failed to be as diligent in teaching responsibility for its use.

Adults, who should certainly know better, are not immune to social media errors that often come back to haunt them. I've always been amazed at how much information people are willing to post. If someone wants my personal information badly enough, I have no doubt it's vulnerable to theft, but let's not *invite* misappropriation.

Don't forget we live in hypersensitive times, and nothing deemed egregious in an unguarded moment is going to receive a pass. Checking an applicant's social media footprint is now common in college admissions and job applications.

In lieu of a standardized etiquette, can we at least practice common sense? Arguing that a comment has been taken out of context rarely proves to be a good defense. The best defense is exercising good judgment in the original post.

Considering whether Grandma would wince at the post is not a bad benchmark to vet contributions to the internet.

Spoogligoo

It's not a real word. I made it up. What does it mean? It's the sound of excuses going on autopilot to justify one's behavior.

I invented this word after breaking up a fight at school. My role was to find out what happened and how the fight started. I turned to the first student and asked for his story. It wasn't an explanation so much as an attempt at playing defense. In the spirit of fair play, I turned to the second student for his story. It was a variation on the same theme. I found myself tuning both out despite my responsibility to get the facts.

When consequences are on the line, the truth is often the first casualty. I do believe each student was telling *his* truth, but it couldn't possibly be close to objective.

I'm not suggesting that you fold your arms, utter the word "spoogligoo," and abandon the negotiation when you suspect a measure of subterfuge at work or in a family discussion. I am recommending, however, that you use the spoogligoo meter to regulate excuse-making in your own arguments.

If you're in a position of mediator, try to temper the personal stakes of those involved. If such is not possible, at least be aware of the dynamics in play. We are all human and this behavior is just one example.

Hear Both What Is Said and What Is Unspoken

There are the words, and then there is the subtext. We've all had conversations where there was so much more swirling just below the surface.

Sometimes, it's hard enough to elicit genuine communication when the participants are on a level playing field. When you introduce a power dynamic, it becomes infinitely harder. This is particularly true if you're in a position of authority like a parent-child relationship or an employer-employee relationship. In this case it's your responsibility to create a safe space for real conversation to occur.

Never defer or deflect because you would rather just not hear it. You're not preventing the conversation—you're simply forcing it underground.

People want to be heard, to be acknowledged, and ultimately

to be respected. These are basic human needs. Do your part by listening. Never underestimate the power of listening. Neither pander nor condescend. *Just listen.*

You may have to make an executive decision. You may see the consequences, the bigger picture, and the bottom line when others cannot. But don't lose your compassion.

Bear in mind that you don't necessarily need to *solve* perceived problems. But do start with lending those problems credence. Often the answers will come naturally from those so wishing to be heard.

Listening is the foundation. The investment you make in trust by listening is incalculable.

TO THE AUTHENTIC
SELF BE TRUE

A Case for Reading Slowly

Students are often surprised to learn that I am not a fast reader. That is by both nature and design. I'm not interested in tearing through a book as though my hair is on fire, especially if the prose is engaging. I want to savor the language as well as the message. Invariably, if I speed up because there are other tasks to be completed (and when are there not) I'm bound to miss something.

The same is true for other endeavors. In fact, the more adept we are at a particular skill, the more invested we become in both the process and the result. In all my years of grading, I never "picked up speed" nor wished to do so. It was partly my own stubbornness that prevented me from inserting preprogrammed feedback because it seemed so impersonal. I don't think anyone's integrity would have been harmed by a computer-generated

"Novel titles require italics, not quotation marks," but somehow writing out the comment gave me a much more intuitive idea of how many students were actually making that particular mistake.

Efficiency has its place, and so does craft.

Are there areas of your life that resist demands for productivity? In other words, you are neither procrastinating nor seeking perfection. You simply want to immerse yourself in the task. If so, you may have just found your true calling. Pay close attention to those projects you relish rather than avoid. They're often found in one's present job or circumstance. In fact, if you're experiencing burnout in your current position, the first order of business is to clarify what parts of the day you actually enjoy. When you can parse those bits from the rest, you may discover a clear vision of what it is you're meant to be doing.

The Essay
and the Argument

The key to composing a compelling literary essay is to create a provable thesis. When analyzing literature, there is no dealing in absolutes. As Mr. Keating says in *Dead Poets Society*, "We're not laying pipe." So, in what way are claims "provable"? One builds an argument through evidence from the text.

When preparing an essay, some students are tempted to write into the abyss, hoping that a thesis will magically appear. It's also common to choose esoteric theories where evidence is lacking. A "what if" scenario is an example of this, as in "What if Frankenstein's monster *wasn't* mistreated?"

Trouble is, anything perfunctory shows its strain. The missing piece is the "So what?" factor. The "Why should I care?" factor. No one wants to read a laundry list of character traits if it leads nowhere—or worse, the tortured ramblings of a student under duress. The goal is to prove something compelling, and hopefully, a bit unexpected.

The "Why should I care?" template is not a bad way to frame any project. Deadlines are a reality, but if they're the only motivation, the final product is likely to be lacking in innovation and sustainability. If you cannot articulate the vision, reconsider the inclination to plod forward while hoping inspiration will unveil itself.

There will be times when we will be required to write proposals, articulate arguments, and make presentations. The same rules apply. Those who honor their audience will know why these communications contain information that is both appealing and necessary. They will also be diligent with integrating the critical data to sell the idea. Invariably, the point of the project will be to solve a problem—whether through restructuring or innovation. All the words on the page or the PowerPoint should support the solution. Even if you have hard data as opposed to literary quotations, there's still a measure of interpretation required to make use of that data in the most persuasive fashion.

Make sure every point you make supports your thesis. Those points and sentences that do not support the thesis are, by definition, derailing it. If the thesis is just a description of the patently obvious, the argument confirms a notion not worth advancing.

Depression

If you want to know what depression feels like, read Emily Dickinson's "There's a certain Slant of light."

There's a certain Slant of light,
Winter Afternoons –
That oppresses, like the Heft
Of Cathedral Tunes –

Heavenly Hurt, it gives us –
We can find no scar,
But internal difference –
Where the meanings, are –

None may teach it – Any –
'Tis the seal Despair –
An imperial affliction

Sent us of the Air –

When it comes, the Landscape listens –
Shadows – hold their breath –
When it goes, 'tis like the Distance
On the look of Death –[4]

I've read many essays, poems, short stories, and novels on the subject. Nothing comes closer.

---

4   *The Poems of Emily Dickinson: Reading Edition*, edited by Ralph W. Franklin (Cambridge, MA: The Belknap Press of Harvard University Press), Copyright © 1998, 1999 by the President and Fellows of Harvard College. Copyright © 1951, 1955 by the President and Fellows of Harvard College. Copyright © renewed 1979, 1983 by the President and Fellows of Harvard College. Copyright © 1914, 1918, 1919, 1924, 1929, 1930, 1932, 1935, 1937, 1942 by Martha Dickinson Bianchi. Copyright © 1952, 1957, 1958, 1963, 1965 by Mary L. Hampson. Used by permission. All rights reserved.

Owning the Work

My students had a "voice" in their writing, their own style of expression. When I read their papers, I could actually hear them posing the argument. That's why a shift in diction, delivery, or phrasing throws up a red flag for instructors: it's a break in the voice. Contrary to popular opinion, English teachers do not take any joy in detecting plagiarism. The minute the breach has been verified through a Google search, all we can see is uncomfortable conversations, more paperwork, and creative consequences. I say creative, because discipline codes are fluid, balanced with teachable moments we hope will take seed.

So often, I realized anew that teachers and students are working at cross purposes. We are assigning essays to assess skills, while they are scrambling to meet a deadline to maintain a grade. The line is not always so decisively drawn, but it's clear enough. It's a divide worth remembering if we wish to teach our children that appropriating material without credit has enduring consequences. It's not just about words—it's also about ideas.

Oh, the stories I could tell you about secondary source material. We as teachers plant the seed of confusion when we ask kids to summarize information by putting it *in their own words.* Suddenly the work has become their own, not simply in defense but with conviction. It can be difficult to convince students that the material still needs to be cited.

Then there are group projects, where the onus of responsibility becomes truly blurred. Although I would ask students to choose partners wisely since their fates were bound, I found myself still struggling with how to properly assess individuals who had clearly done more than their fair share and those who had done far less. Unless an imbalance was egregious, the members usually shared the grade, as I imagine happens in the corporate world. If you put Type A and slackers together and they beat the system by playing to their "strengths," as it were, what skills are we truly reinforcing?

LIVING GRACEFULLY

The UFO Ball

I used to do an experiment with willing students. It involved a circle, holding hands, and an educational tool called a UFO ball that resembled a ping-pong ball with two thin silver strips. If the group all held hands and I held the ball, two kids could each put their index fingers on the respective silver strips, and the ball would make a noise like a tuning fork and flicker. (This last step took some coaxing and assurances that I was not attempting to thin the herd.) If one set of students unclasped their hands, it would fail to work.

An unbroken circle can do many things, but if just one fails to cooperate, the magic will fade.

Put the Kettle On

Never underestimate the power of the "cuppa." When I was growing up, a cup of tea was the answer to both major and minor upsets, private or public.

Will tea solve the problem? Surprisingly, it often does. It's a time to pause, reflect, journal, engage in deep conversation, or take part in a lively chat. It's a civilized and a civilizing tradition.

When preparing tea, the key is to bring the water to a rolling boil before immersing the tea bag, and to not be stingy with the steep. If planning to use milk or cream, add it to the cup first. This way, you'll always make sufficient room and successfully infuse the liquids.

If you have time to properly celebrate, consider using a China teacup or adding a biscuit. Unless you're entertaining royalty, dunking is permitted. It's really about giving yourself time to put things in perspective—either with yourself or someone else.

If You Don't Know, Say So

There's no shame in saying "I don't know." If you feel you owe your audience more, then make a vow to find out. You're not going to resolve anything by digging yourself in further.

Avoid using phrases that fill the void but add nothing to the conversation.

Resist the urge to bury inconvenient truths in language that is confusing or misleading. Being forthright is refreshing and invites trust. Honesty is not a weakness, it's an asset. So is humility. Nothing inspires confidence in others so much as candor.

How Far We Fall is up to You, Not the Calendar

When I was a kid, I used to think one peaked at the age of 25, or 30 if the gods were generous. From there, it was just a precipitous descent to the inevitable. Standing far on the other side of this divide, I'm happy to report my prediction was not at all accurate. One plateaus physically, which is not particularly sexy, I suppose, but it is far better than decline.

To go the distance, it becomes increasingly important to take care of the body we are given. On that topic, I would like to suggest we all start simplifying the equations. While maintaining health may not be adequately summed up by "eat less and move more," we have, in this country, made the conversation unnecessarily difficult. There are scientific and cultural recommendations offered in the hopes of either narrowing or expanding the possibilities of what good health looks like. We can listen to the recognized gurus, our own intuition, or to a combination of both. But let's have a goal of moderation and good sense that we can manage and model for our own children.

Whole foods, in their purest form, have the most nutrients to offer. This doesn't mean you have to go raw, but do aim for a colorful plate with plenty of fruits and vegetables. Find ways to move your body and celebrate its miraculous design. You may sign up for classes with coaches but remember that you can exercise this magnificent structure just as easily on your own and for free.

Put simply, use what you were given and apply proper maintenance. Do this for yourself first and foremost, and then for those you love who deserve your time. Set goals if you wish, but do not impose edicts that are unsustainable and joyless.

The Lady Doth Protest Too Much

I have noticed that people are increasingly offended and easily outraged. It's evident on social media, in cable news, and throughout public discourse. There's an unmistakable anger that permeates commentary.

That level of wrath, however righteous, reduces reactions to binaries. You are with us or against us. You either get it or you don't. The pandemic has created both hardship and opportunities for reflection. It has underscored longstanding inequities and brought them into painfully sharp focus. If ever there was a time for opportunity to spring from crisis, it's now. Unfortunately, there's no shortage of voices shouting to be heard. Struggle is radical by definition and rarely polite since that which has become institutionalized is slow to change—if willing to budge at all. Yet, it's getting harder to recognize movements that are pure of spirit, as many seem more preoccupied with staking a claim rather than effecting true change.

Don't Support the Plastic Parrot Industry

Since I rose at 4:15 a.m. each morning for work, I would sometimes turn on the television for company. This is prime time for infomercials and advertising products of questionable value. One such example is Perfect Polly, a motion-activated plastic parrot that chirps. The true abomination, however, was the marketing. Here's the scenario: You have an elderly relative who lives alone. They don't want the trouble and cost of a pet, but they are desperately lonely. When you're in need of a solution, send them this hunk of plastic to fool them into forgetting they're alone.

Let's not do this to our elders. Let's not do this to anyone. If you're confused about a gift, do not give a motion-activated hunk of plastic. Consider a handwritten letter or a phone call instead.

Make Your Apologies Mean Something

If you choose to apologize, do so sincerely. If the best you can muster is, "I'm sorry that you're upset," perhaps you should say nothing.

I always wondered why parents and principals directed misbehaving students to write letters of apology as penance. No one wants a letter of apology sent under duress.

If you stand by what you said or did, then perhaps the question to ask is, "How do we move forward?" This statement demonstrates that you value the relationship. Sending *that* message is the important and abiding one.

Never Refuse the Kindness of a Quarter

There's a wonderful tradition at the Aldi supermarket where people hand over their cart to the next person without removing the quarter it takes to initially secure it. Now, do some abuse the custom? Yes. I once saw a young man take a string of quarters out of the carts to put toward a pack of cigarettes. I know this because he announced it to his companion. As he walked by me, I said, "You don't want to take them all; that invites bad karma." I said it calmly and with a smile. He nodded to me and put one back.

Sometimes the reaction to proffered help can be mixed because it isn't necessarily *needed*. My female colleagues, many of whom were 20 years my junior, have proclaimed that they resent men offering to help them with heavy packages. I get it. I just don't agree. If a gentleman offers me help, I'm touched by the kindness, not offended by a perceived helplessness. I once blew a tire on the Interstate in Alabama. I'd barely pulled my pickup to the shoulder before a trucker stopped and offered to change the tire. I accepted that offer with gratitude.

Nobody Is Looking

I have many favorite lines from *Hamlet*. One of my top contenders is, "There are more things in heaven and earth, Horatio, than are dreamt of in your philosophy" (Act 1, Scene 5). While this one inspires wonder in what we do not yet understand, there are plenty of others that remind us of our own mortality. I'm not even talking about the obvious choice that contemplates being or not being.

I'm not here to speculate on what comes next, only to treasure what's happening now.

It's time to stop worrying about what other people think. Chances are quite good they're not thinking of us at all.

By all means, honor and protect your good name. That's where your responsibility ends. The opinions of others are neither your concern nor an area where you can exert much control.

I hope no one is still trying to keep up with the Joneses. Own your choices and your tastes. Ironically, nothing impresses others more.

Granting Grace

I taught for four years at a Catholic school in St. Mary Parish in Louisiana. During the last period of the day, we had the opportunity to recite the act of contrition. I'm not a Catholic, so my understanding of the practice was certainly more secular than religious, but I appreciated it nonetheless. For me, it was a time to pause and reflect about the day and identify where I could improve.

The custom of being humbled was refreshing. There was always the promise of tomorrow and the chance to make it better. I often wish there were such a moment of reset in modern-day life. It would not necessarily be about penance for a sin or submission to one's maker, though it could be. What we would all benefit from is an acknowledgment that none of us has all the answers and that success may be preceded by a fair amount of stumbling.

SERENDIPITOUS STUFF

The Great Idea
(We Never Pursue)

When I taught ninth graders, I had a plush toy on my desk. It was actually a giant purple Peep. Students were allowed to use it as a stress reliver if they were anxious or upset. One day, my colleague Diane, a biology teacher, entered my classroom, gave the Peep a sound mashing, and exited without a word.

Diane noticed that since it had been squeezed so many times, the Peep was wonderfully malleable, and after school she took great delight in coming up with funny characters, which we named "gangsta Peep," "misanthrope Peep," and so on.

We always said we should write a book featuring our cast of characters. But, we reasoned, the Peep is copyrighted. So, we kept making up characters for our own amusement only.

And then the unthinkable happened. A horrified Diane brought a book entitled *Peeps: A Candy-Coated Tale*, populated with a bunch of Peep "characters," some clearly irreverent, to my classroom. What are the chances? Turns out, better than we think. While I still have a hard time believing Diane and I could have successfully pitched the idea to a publishing house, it had indeed been done by two more enterprising than we.

The book still sits on my shelf, a reminder of what could have been. It holds Diane's simple inscription of "We've been scooped."

Don't sit on your ideas and invent reasons for their unviability. If a particular notion resonates, give it some time and attention. You may be taken down a new path. You may find added momentum. You may get turned down. But do yourself a favor and honor the insight.

The Parking Lot

Dealing with the public is good experience for young people. One of my earliest jobs was as a parking lot attendant. Mind you, this wasn't even a valet gig. I just took money at the gate and oversaw the lot. But people are their authentic selves while parking the car. How do people act when there's no one to impress and nothing to be gained? It's revealing of character.

When the lot got busy, I would direct people to specific spots. This was to ease the flow of traffic, as there was only one entrance and exit. Most were accommodating, but some would bristle.

Sometimes I had to insist that people correct sloppy parking. Most responded appropriately to the instruction, but some would only do so after expressing great consternation over the inconvenience. On occasion, someone would hand me a $10 bill and then insist they had given me $20. Others would dump garbage on the lot.

However, the most common customer incivility was ignoring

me as I stood dutifully by the gate trying to receive them. They would drive into the lot without stopping to pay and simply take matters into their own hands. These same people would thrust the cash in my general direction only as an afterthought without even making eye contact.

If you want a quick barometer for someone's set of values, observe how they treat people in the service industry. This includes wait staff, cashiers, gas station attendants, etc.

Let's agree—for instance—to stay off the phone when talking to people serving us. They're not an incidental in your life. Why should others be subjected to your attempt at multitasking? Nothing communicates "I'm important and you're not" faster than this behavior. Being present honors everyone involved.

Everyone Needs a Pit Crew

When I broke my wrist, it was the middle of the night. I didn't want to call an ambulance because I didn't want to deprive someone who was having a heart attack of emergency care. After all, my arm wasn't going to get any more broken. But I didn't feel sufficiently comfortable driving myself to the hospital.

So, what do I do? Who should I call? I quickly ran through a short list. Not my elderly neighbor who on occasion watched my cat. Not a colleague who had a rare opportunity to sleep in. My friend Johnny was the only option. Why? Because Johnny didn't panic or ask unnecessary questions. He grabbed the phone on the first ring and sounded as if he had been awake for hours. I explained the situation and he said he'd be right over. *That's* the person you call.

There's plenty of time after the crisis is over to second-guess and conduct mop-up operations. In the moment, what you need is a level head and a calm response.

If you can establish this arrangement before the emergency arises, there will be one less detail to consume your precious energy during the disaster.

The Frontal Lobe

This part of the brain is in charge of managing higher-level executive functions, including decision-making and impulse control. The prefrontal cortex does not become fully developed until the age of 25.[5] Think about that for a minute. It explains a lot, doesn't it?

Sometimes when young people say they don't know why they did something, they're not being evasive. Sometimes, they really don't know. Yes, it perhaps did seem like a good idea at the time. No, they weren't necessarily thinking about the consequences, even though they may appear obvious to you.

I used to tell my students that if they wanted to be treated like the adults they were becoming, they had to demonstrate they were ready to be trusted with the big things. In other words, instead of demanding more freedom, demonstrate your readi-

5   Mariam Arain et al., "Maturation of the adolescent brain,"
    Neuropsychiatric Disease and Treatment 9 (2013): 449–461, https://
    www.doi.org/10.2147/NDT.S39776.

ness to be free. While I still believe in holding kids accountable, I have become much more mindful of the science behind why they do what they do.

The Story of the Good Dancer

You may not be old enough to remember after school specials. The show was cutting edge in the '80s, tackling previously taboo subjects like suicide and eating disorders. For some reason, one scene in particular has stayed with me. In the episode, there was an old widow who was giving dating advice to a teenaged girl. It went something like this:

Old Widow: "My dear, there are two kinds of men in the world. The good dancers and the bad dancers. You will meet both at the high school dance. The good dancer is popular and confident. All the girls want to be with him; all the boys want to *be* him. When he whirls you around the dance floor, you feel like you are floating on air and imagine all who see you are filled with envy."

"The bad dancer is the boy by the punch bowl who is too shy to ask you to dance. If you do manage to cajole him, the experience will be a disaster. He won't look at you, and you will have to work hard not to have your feet trodden upon."

Girl: "The popular boy would never notice me."

Old Widow: "If you marry the good dancer, you will appear to have won the lottery. And for a while, the relationship will be happy. But with time and in the face of obstacles, he will put himself first and wonder why you are holding him back. If you are lucky enough to marry the bad dancer, you will know and love a man that will walk beside you through all the good times and bad. He will support you and fight for you and cry with you and champion your goals in life. His love will grow over time, and you will be amazed at the endless stores of passion and devotion he holds within."

Girl: "Wow, you must have had a wonderful marriage and a loving husband."

Old Widow: "I wouldn't know, my dear. I married a good dancer."

I used to tell this story to my students before the first dance of the year with the caveat that good dancers are not selfish. But there is something to be said for allowing people to grow into their finest selves without allowing our own limiting beliefs to define what we see.

Signature Dish

My cooking abilities are limited. My baking is a bit better but nothing to brag about. However, I need not show up empty-handed to a dinner party or barbecue, as I have a signature dish that is always a favorite. It's my fruit salad.

When people offer to bring fruit, they often show up with a wheel of various melon wedges and a dipping sauce. So, I shall impart to you my fruit salad recipe, passed down by my mother.

The key to a wonderful fruit salad, no matter the season, is the base. The secret ingredient is canned peaches in heavy syrup. Do not cut corners here or reach for a "healthy" alternative. The rest of the fruit will be as fresh as nature intended. But the base must be peaches in heavy syrup, used sparingly and well.

Directions:

→ Pour some of the heavy syrup into a large serving bowl.

→ Add the slices of hearty fruits, such as apples and pears.

→ Next add in the oranges, grapefruit, or other citrus fruits. Mix gently.

→ Now come the peaches, grapes, plums, and berries. Mix once again with a gentle hand.

→ Garnish with kiwi or (my personal favorite) star fruit. (The slices make stars!)

→ Reserve a bit of the heavy syrup for a glisten just before serving.

The goal here is for the person who gets the last serving to have the same experience as the person who eats the first bowl. Modify as necessary in the winter. I'm a big proponent of eating with the seasons. You may substitute cantaloupe, honeydew, and watermelon. However, if you want this dish to be memorable, do not make it the main attraction. This is a dish that tastes even better the second day.

Missteps When Upset and/or *Hangry*

One Friday after a long week at work, I had a singular mission at the deli counter at Wawa, my local convenience store. They have the best mac and cheese, bar none, in the world.

I was waiting in gleeful anticipation when a young man walked in with his girlfriend and began screaming at her with colorful expletives.

I'd like to say I was appalled that this woman was being accosted, or simply that one human being was mistreating another. But that would not be true. I was tired, hungry, and my ears were being assailed. I simply wanted it to stop. So, in a fit of self-righteous indignation, I summoned all the venom I could muster, turned to him, and said, "Why don't you give it a rest?"

This six-foot-tall, angry 20-something man hissed back, "Lady, don't you *mess* with me. You have no idea what I'm capable of."

A wiser woman would have let the incident go. But I was tired and hungry, and I wasn't willing to settle for a world where I would be thwarted in my modest efforts to procure some Wawa mac and cheese on a Friday night.

So, I turned to him and said in an icy voice, "Oh, I think your cards are pretty much on the table. But you have no idea what *I* am capable of." What did that even mean? I had no cards up my sleeve to play.

As soon as the words had escaped my lips, I knew I had made a colossal mistake. The guy was seething with anger but frustrated in his efforts to decide on an acceptable response. The only thing that saved me was being a middle-aged woman.

It was a ridiculous standoff. The mutual glare was broken by my mac and cheese being served. I grabbed it and made a quick exit.

So, what's the point? Here I am, a mature, self-respecting (middle-aged) woman, and it was so easy to lose my cool. I was pissed and hangry and filled with self-entitlement.

I share this story with my students because I want them to remember it the next time they are tempted to settle the score for a light slight. There is always at least one unknown variable: the emotional state of the other person. In the heat of the moment, even reasonable people are capable of incredibly foolish actions.

I'm reminded once again of Curley from *Of Mice and Men*. Never back a man (or woman) into a corner. If they're inclined to save face through anger, they will undoubtedly leave that corner through you.

Tony's Words of Wisdom

Tony and his wife, Annie, are friends of mine who live in Brooklyn. He's Italian and she's Sicilian. They are quintessential Brooklynites. Yes, "fuhgeddaboudit" comes to them naturally.

Tony is normally very animated and a master storyteller. One evening when I joined them for dinner, Annie convinced a somewhat reluctant Tony to share his act of generosity at a local restaurant.

"Yeah, Annie and I were having dinner and across the dining room there was this family. You know, mom, dad, a bunch of kids. And I could see that, you know, this family was down on its luck."

In essence, when Tony paid for his and Annie's meal, he directed the server to send him the family's bill as well. He discreetly paid both bills and left the restaurant.

"And then what happened?"

"Whaddaya mean?"

"Well, how did the family react?"

Then came the words of wisdom that have stayed with me. "When you do something nice for someone, you don't stick around. Ya do and ya go."

Tony explained that he didn't want the moment to be awkward or the father to feel as if he couldn't provide for his family. He just wanted the moment *to be*.

Just let the moment be. "Ya do and ya go."

THE CURVEBALLS IN LIFE

The Fall Would Probably Kill You, and What I Learned in the Army, Part I

When I was in the Reserve Officers' Training Corps in college, one of our assignments was to walk to the end of the high diving board in full battle dress uniform with a rifle. Blindfolded. We were instructed to walk down the board with our arms outstretched holding the rifle, so that when we hit the water, we would not hit ourselves with the weapon under the chin and break our own necks.

Why, you ask?

This is what my platoon sergeant said. "If you were traveling through enemy territory at night and you fell off a cliff, the fall would probably kill you. But if you were lucky enough to fall into a body of water, you certainly wouldn't want to break your neck if there was a chance you could swim to shore."

Why would anyone travel through enemy territory in pitch darkness?

These and other questions remained unanswered.

I am proud of the opportunity to serve my country, though it was admittedly limited in scope. It also served as a primer for the by turns amorphous and exacting nature of large organizations. I would later experience this phenomenon in school districts. "We do it this way because we have always done it this way."

In the Army, there's an esprit de corps that covers a multitude of incongruences. This is decidedly less true in corporations, even the non-profit ones. While there are well-intentioned people in the ranks and even at the helm, at times you may wonder.

Flexibility and patience serve well under these circumstances.

What I Learned in The Army, Part II

When you rappel, you don't just get harnessed and jump backwards off a cliff. You have to get parallel with the mountain before you bound off it. Initially, this runs counter to every fiber of your being. We prefer to look forward, not to cantilever ourselves over the abyss. However, not taking this step is a recipe for smashing your face into the mountain.

So, what's the lesson?

Before undertaking the task, do your research. There may be fundamental steps that sound counterintuitive to the novice, but these same foundational steps are going to support an entire journey.

Do Something That Scares You

Here's the litmus test: Consider the worst thing that could happen if you do this thing. If the worst thing is a felony conviction, abort the mission. However, if the worst thing that can happen is embarrassment, you might want to seriously consider it.

When I was in graduate school, doing something that scared me was an assignment—to teach a lesson out of our discipline and comfort level. The professor wanted us to feel like struggling students.

Teachers should never forget that for some, the classroom is a scary and frustrating place. As a student, my nemesis was math. I'd mastered basic computation well enough to balance a checkbook. But Geometry was a complete mystery. Absolutely nothing was intuitive. I still don't know how I got through Calculus.

I suspect my teacher took pity on me.

So, what did I choose to do to face my fear? I chose to explain a math problem in front in my peers. I described the movement of a Ferris wheel and the trigonometry involved.

I prepared for that lesson by being tutored one-on-one, so I had the time on my own terms to understand the concepts involved. In fact, the movement of a Ferris wheel challenges assumptions about movement over time. There was a natural hook to introducing the lesson and answering the "why should I care" question. It was so gratifying to turn the tide on the emotions I had long associated with mathematics.

Why harbor anxiety about something if you have the power to change your associations with it? If you have avoided a subject for years, it may look very different now. At the very least, *you have the ability to change* what it looks like now.

Meeting Your Idols

My favorite television series growing up was *Starsky and Hutch*. It was a show about two plainclothes detectives who flouted most of the rules but never their integrity while solving crime in the fictional Bay City. It may have had a fair bit of violence, and it certainly carries a painfully dated '70s style, for better or for worse. But in other ways it was quite progressive, never shying away from storylines about race, sexual orientation, and the downtrodden. My particular attraction arose from the good-looking costars, Paul Michael Glaser and David Soul, and their natural onscreen chemistry.

When I got my first computer in graduate school, the first thing I typed in the search engine was "Starsky and Hutch" in hopes of catching a glimpse of my memories. What I discovered was a thriving world of conventions and fanfic. What a strange and nerdy and wonderful discovery! I started writing to another fan named Carol who lived in Boston and met Glaser as a teenager. She spoke wistfully of her hope to one day meet Glaser and Soul together.

Five years went by, and one day when I was back home in Pennsylvania with a full-time teaching position, I got an unexpected email from Carol. There had been buzz about a *Starsky and Hutch* remake film starring Ben Stiller and Owen Wilson, but Carol was solely focused on realizing a childhood dream: meeting the original actors from the series together. She suggested we fly out to Hollywood in the hopes of catching sight of the two on the red carpet at the film's premiere. My first reaction was that this was silly. Can one just *go* to the red carpet? If so, how would we get anywhere near the actors? Carol quickly reminded me that she was also a teacher and additionally had a husband and three children, one of whom had special needs. If she could go, I could certainly make arrangements with my job *and for my cat*. I know when I've been outmaneuvered.

So, I flew to Los Angeles to meet Carol. Unbeknownst to me, our mutual friend, Terri, had sent an email to the newly aired *On Air with Ryan Seacrest* show. The show's premise was introducing diehard fans to their idols. Terri's email caught the attention of the producers, and before I knew what was happening, Carol and I were invited onto the show.

What came next was a whirlwind. Carol impressed Ryan with her Boston accent and 29-year commitment to a show. Carol was pinned as interviewer and I as videographer, and we were given center stage on the red carpet to interview all the stars. But our hearts were with two in particular. We were given '70s outfits from Wasteland, a hip vintage store, and got to speak to David Soul and Paul Michael Glaser. We confirmed that their onscreen chemistry had turned into a lifelong friendship. It was quite a moment.

I planned to keep the whole thing a secret. However, that was not to be. A secretary from my school happened to catch the episode. She greeted me in the office with, "That was you, wasn't it?" Word spread quickly around the Freshman Center.

So, I started showing clips of my 15 minutes of fame to my students as proof that if the worst thing that can happen is simple embarrassment, you should probably do it. For the record, they were far more impressed that I had met Snoop Dogg.

Shadow Boxers

In Ayn Rand's *The Fountainhead*, there's a character named Lois Cook who is an aspiring writer. She is the author of a book entitled *The Gallant Gallstone*, which is touted as literary genius but is, in reality, largely unreadable. Elsworth Toohey, a book promoter, knows the book is trash, but he is determined to demonstrate his own power to influence public taste.

In real life, there are those who are flaunted as experts by those who know very little. And there are those who talk a good game but fail to deliver. My father refers to such people as the shadow boxers. I am generally open to listen to what anyone has to say, but I've always been suspicious of charismatic folk. That is patently unfair, I know, but they make me nervous. I always feel like they're trying to sell me something. And like the bullies of the world, they walk among us.

I prefer to err on the side of compassion, but just make sure that in a relationship where something tangible is to be gained, someone is not simply on the take. There is nothing wrong with selling a product, so long as we're not talking about a scam. You don't want to add bad juju or karma to the earthly plain. In a perfect world, an exchange is mutually beneficial. It is "give and take," not "take and take more."

Our Kin

When I graduated from high school, my parents threw me a party at my uncle's restaurant. My uncle, in turn, invited half a dozen ex-girlfriends to the celebration and sat them all at the same table. My father invited a bunch of ironworker buddies who imbibed more than recommended until one of them, most likely my dad, came up with the idea of climbing the water tower behind the restaurant. My friends and I got a front-row seat to adults behaving badly. The ex-girlfriends hissed, the boisterous boys scaled the tower, and both groups egged each other on with colorful expletives. My mother was no doubt wondering when and where things had gone so terribly wrong. My uncle gave me a sloppy kiss, which I did not appreciate, and $200 in cash, which I did.

Ah, families and relatives. We don't get to choose them. They will, however, weave themselves into the stories of our lives. When I was growing up, my mother never used to tell my father and me her sisters were coming to visit until about 20 minutes before their arrival. I found them delightful, but as my father was more inclined to believe, there was a sisterhood dynamic that was less than welcoming to outsiders. They had that short-hand way of speaking that siblings often do.

After a holiday break, my students would regale the class with amusing stories. There were traditional celebrations and predictable squabbles that are so much more entertaining when they are happening to someone else's family.

These relationships can be fragile, and when we think of the unpacking we *could* do, it gives us pause. Often there's a balance of affection and obligation. We balance what we want to say with what will never be said.

Here's my simple advice: Go easy on them, and go easy on yourself.

People

Yes, they walk among us. They will both disappoint and amaze you. You need to embrace them, forgive them, set boundaries with them, and hold them accountable. They are strong and fragile, unpredictable, and irritatingly familiar. There will come a day when someone you love dearly will say something that will take your breath away. It may be good or bad, but either way, it will be stunning.

We are all flawed humans. We know this intellectually, but the heart is slower to accept the fact. We can make sacrifices for those we love, but not in a way that robs us of our own spirit. Those around us may offer advice, but ultimately, we will make the decision to stay, to go, or to compromise. Choose with your head and your heart but go easy on yourself. These choices are difficult to make with both polarities in play.

MANAGING THE
HARD STUFF

"This Too Shall Pass"

My mother loved to utter the words to the title of this passage. As with many proffered words of advice, the wisdom has revealed itself only over time. They are powerful words, and they are often true.

When misfortune befalls and you have done what you can in the moment to address it, ask yourself how important the event will be five days, five months, or five years from now. When we're young, it's harder to properly prioritize upsets. With time and experience, we grow more adept at recognizing levels of urgency. We learn to pace ourselves to navigate the immediate, daily, and chronic setbacks.

It's such an inconvenient irony that the lessons we need to learn early on come through hard-won experience and the passage of time. If my mature self could speak to my younger self, would I appreciate the advice or resent the intrusion? Probably the latter.

Choosing Your Battles

There are situations that must elicit a choice.

This is not going to be a deep conversation. But there is a connection to the wiles of human nature.

Near my home is a busy intersection, Route 202 and Route 413. My destination is not 413—I am committed to 202. However, shortly after this turn, 202 comes to a T. Trying to make the left a block later is nerve-racking, so I travel to a turn that is supported by a light.

Route 202 has a wide shoulder with lines through it, indicating we should not drive on the shoulder. But it's so very wide and accommodating, and it does seem to support the flow of traffic, particularly at rush hour, to use this shoulder to get a head start on the right-hand turn.

One day, however, there must have been an incident. On my drive home, an official-looking, angry sign had been posted about staying off the shoulder, and a cop was stationed at the intersection. I'm sure it was not actually an "angry" sign, but the message was clear and we all stayed in our lane. A couple days after that, the cop disappeared. A few days later, the sign was removed. And then those of us making the right-hand turn had a choice to make.

We knew the rule, we had been reminded of the rule, and now we were left to our own devices to do the right thing. At first, we were tentative, and then someone got bold, and then, once again, we were all using the shoulder. I noticed two things about my own reaction. I happily returned to the shoulder because doing so eased the flow of traffic, but I also realized that it just wasn't in me to follow the rules in this instance. Sometimes there are no good choices, so we just settle for the path of least resistance.

Avoid Golden Handcuffs

The expression "golden handcuffs" refers to a situation that's comfortable. For example, let's say you have a job that offers health insurance. It's not fulfilling, but it pays the bills and provides security. Perhaps it's not just you who are offered that security but your family as well.

In this situation, it's best to be careful of settling into the well-worn path without some introspection about the possibilities before you. Perhaps it's not time to leave your job, but it's always the right time to begin living a more fulfilling life.

This is also a good philosophy to model for your children. If you aren't happy, you owe it to yourself and to those you love to figure out why without fear of discovering the answer. It can be scary to be fully present because you're forced to admit things you would rather not see. But acquiescing is only a short-term solution. What you reap in safety may be a down payment on regret.

The Rule of Seven

I've always been a procrastinator. I generally get the task done, but often not without a sizable measure of angst. Perhaps this sounds familiar. No judgment.

The issue is I typically spend an inordinate amount of time *thinking* about what I need to do. Like regret, this is an empty investment. There's doing and not doing—and then there's simply mulling over the doing with a guilty conscience. Making lists is helpful and may prioritize your responsibilities, but it certainly does not complete them.

One labor-intensive task that I faced during my teaching career was grading essays. I wanted to give written feedback that was supportive and constructive, not simply circle comma splices with an angry red pen. I also felt a responsibility to showcase writing when it was impressive. It could be a passage or simply a turn of phrase. Well, that takes time, and getting started was the hard part. Once in the flow of grading, the momentum builds. But oh, the getting started.

There's a psychological term used in education known as "chunking," which involves breaking down a large and imposing assignment into manageable pieces. It works for completing the assignment, and equally well for grading those assignments. After all, grading 120 essays is a daunting task, but only grading seven essays is much more manageable. It's a riff on that notion a journey of a thousand miles begins with a single step. Why seven, you ask? The number is arbitrary, but it works. The progress is measurable, and multiples of seven add up surprisingly quickly.

And then there are the rewards! Grade seven, make a cup of tea. Grade seven more, watch a YouTube video. Or, if one is very lucky, the seven may just turn into 20. You can apply this method to organizing, delegating, communicating, cleaning, etc. Just be sure to celebrate your progress.

Red Ribbon Week

There's a designated week in October known as Red Ribbon Week. It's part of an anti-drug campaign aimed at public high schools. Students are asked to wear red ribbons or stickers that read "I am drug free." While I believe that schools are delivering an important message, I would often worry about Red Ribbon Week becoming an obligatory exercise with limited enduring value. When I asked students how this campaign had gotten started, few could tell me it was in honor of Enrique "Kiki" Camarena, an officer in the Drug Enforcement Administration killed in the line of duty.

At one school where I taught, there was a scheduled assembly from the sheriff's department that showed the aftermath of overdoses. At one time, officers would roll out body bags in front of the students. This graphic scare tactic served a purpose, but I preferred to share the story of my stepsister, Patty, who died many years ago.

In the 1980s, Patty built an impressive career for herself on Wall Street. Unfortunately, the stress of her job and the lifestyle of Manhattan led to a cocaine habit that blossomed into a heroin addiction. By the time I met her, the consequences of long-term drug use had become clear. We thought a nasty infection at an injection site on her leg would serve as her rock bottom, if there is such a thing. My stepmother would hear stories from the neighborhood about Patty riding the E train at four in the morning, nodding out. And then one day Patty just disappeared without a trace. She may have overdosed or have been met with foul play. We shall likely never know.

Patty's struggle seemed over, but for her mother, Eva, the pain of the loss was just beginning, and was accompanied by the attendant guilt and regret. Eva would always wonder if her own demons had predisposed her daughter to addiction.

For many years, when I called my father in Brooklyn, I would hear Eva's instructions to leave a message. This was followed by a special message for Patty, assuring her that she was loved and that she needed to call home. My father once approached me about convincing Eva to change the message. He found it unsettling and even embarrassing. I told him that I had no intention of having that conversation with a grieving mother who had lost her only child. Only Eva could decide when it was time to change the message.

One day, many years later, I called to discover Eva had changed the message. She had made her peace with the fact that Patty was gone and that closure would be denied. Still, after many more years, Eva continues to carry the pain in her heart.

This is the story I told my students during Red Ribbon Week.

It didn't focus solely on Patty—it focused also on Eva and the family left behind. For those left behind are also part of the horror of drug addiction.

Teenagers often feel invincible. They are impressionable, curious, and subject to levels of peer pressure of which adults are largely unaware. When I taught seniors, their minds were looking ahead to college and new adventures, and perhaps experimentation. I resisted taglines like "Just say no." I talked about never willingly giving up one's own sense of agency in a world that is no stranger to crimes of opportunity. I spoke about the body being a sacred vessel that needs to last a lifetime through all our choices. And I described Eva's phone message. That message hits home in the way that Kiki Camarena's story does. It speaks to enduring loss.

If you want to speak to your children about drugs, don't just speak about the dangers of using. Speak about the family who would be left behind.

Regret

If you hold compassion and empathy in your heart, you run the risk of experiencing regret. Just so we're clear, you *want* to hold compassion and empathy in your heart. Our feelings regulate our behavior. Getting the heart and head to work in tandem is sometimes a tall order, but it's also a sign of our humanity. Regret is the one you want to avoid.

Regret develops when you deny yourself forgiveness. It's usually tied to failing to listen to our better selves. Regret can be a motivator, but it's such a deep-seated, self-incriminating emotion that once we enter its grips it has the consistency of quicksand. That's why you want to avoid it. Regret is an unrelenting taskmaster. And unless you plan to use the story of your regret as a cautionary tale for others, it only robs you of potential joy.

If your fragile sensibility is ravaged by this animal, what do you think five, 10, or 25 more years of suffering is going to look and feel like? If you're overwhelmed, then invite others into the healing process. If you cannot make amends with a person who has passed, then extend the olive branch to yourself.

There are many things I would do differently if given a chance, but that's not how the game is played. The fact that time in our physical bodies is finite also enhances the rhythm of the journey. We are knitting the story as we go, and only in retrospect are some of the patterns visible. Anne Lamott says that people are "so ruined, and so loved, and in charge of so little."[6] I love that idea and find it empowering.

As Hemingway said, we have the potential to be "strong at the broken places."[7] Regret, however, only wants us to wallow and to replay the imagined mistake over and over at a higher and higher frequency. You cannot learn from your mistakes if you become entrenched in them. Make your peace. Make the world a bit lighter.

6   Anne Lamott, *Help, Thanks, Wow: The Three Essential Prayers* (New York: Riverhead Books, 2012), 27.

7   Ernest Hemingway, *A Farewell to Arms* (Jupiter, FL: Pharos Books, 2022), 249.

Managing Grief

There's no right way or wrong way to grieve. Sometimes you get stuck or mistakenly believe you have finally resolved your sadness. The holidays are a challenge you may see coming, only to be caught by an unanticipated moment that reminds you of your lost loved one. Once you realize that grief is not something that you have to put behind you, the more manageable it becomes.

I lost my mother to suicide in my 20s. I felt a range of emotions I could barely identify, let alone reconcile. I recognize now that I spent a fair amount of time vacillating between depression and rage. My father, being English, was loving and supportive but not emotive, so navigating this territory was foreign and frightening for me. An early lesson is that anger feels better than anguish because you don't feel quite as helpless and depleted. What a hollow realization.

In an attempt to be proactive about my struggle, when I began my teaching career in Louisiana I sought out a grief counselor and later a priest. The same analogy kept emerging: the one about the tapestry that encourages us to look at our lives from a broader perspective of grace. To be honest, I was only half listening. *There are no answers. My life is in knots. I am miserable. I have nothing to offer.* I began to believe that despair was my new normal and my mother's death would simply divide my life into two parts. In Part II, I would remain unrecognizable to myself.

However, I kept hearing the story about the tapestry, so I figured it held some significance for me. One day, I got it during a discussion with my students. In essence, one's present misery is like the back of the tapestry, which seems a cruel jumble of strands without direction or significance. It's only with time that the front of the woven masterpiece is revealed. It is then that the heartache takes its rightful and measured place in the story of a life, a beautiful life. Not a fragile life marred by tragedy.

I missed my mother terribly, and there were questions that would never be sufficiently answered. But more than anything else, I was scared that I had lost myself. That I would be forever looking at the world through a veil of sadness. It seemed as if my grief and guilt had taken on unmanageable dimensions.

I did not share with my students whom I had lost or in what manner. What I did share is that I got stuck in the sorrow of the loss, to the point that I believed I had lost myself. What I did share with them, I'll now share with you. You will always be you. Your essence is intact. The keys to finding perspective are time and perhaps the counsel of others. You will laugh heartily again and will know joy even if it currently feels out of reach.

The authentic *you* who is capable of a range of emotions and a towering strength is waiting to greet an old friend.

Unexpected Lessons

I'm going to tell you something else I did not share with my students. I was a victim of sexual assault. Okay, let's call it what it is: rape. I did not know my attacker, but I did have the opportunity to look him straight in the eye, albeit through a drugged haze. What I saw was pure, unadulterated hatred. Not evil but hate.

Surprisingly, in that moment were the seeds of my healing. I did not experience that healing immediately. But that moment would offer me perspective, which is often the answer to trauma.

I do not pretend that I have the answer to surviving violence. This is not #MeToo. There is neither a playbook nor a timeline for getting over or beyond pain. If someone suggests that there is, I can guarantee that the idea will make you angry and resentful.

My intent is only to share with you what I saw when I looked into those hateful eyes. I saw an open, bleeding wound. It didn't justify what was happening. As most of us know by now, rape is not a crime of passion. It is a crime of rage. There's no action that will satisfy that level of anger. It is not extinguished—it is only fed. What I discovered in those eyes was that whatever happened to me that night, I would never be hurt like that man had been hurt. These are not platitudes that I fed to myself, and I felt that truth.

I felt violated, and I experienced anger, but I never experienced shame. I never felt that something had been stripped from me that I would never get back. The depravity in that face did not fill me with enduring distress but instead left me with sadness. I somehow imagined that he saw this in my eyes too. I cannot imagine pity was what he either expected or could stand.

In life there will be defining moments, not to be confused with forging identity. I could have chosen to look at the world as a darker and more menacing place. My world could have become smaller as I retreated from it. That behavior wouldn't have honored the lesson of moving forward.

Navigating the Past

Make your peace. **Make** your peace. Make your peace.

You need not forget the past nor relegate it to a safe space. You don't have to scatter forgiveness with "cool patience," as Queen Gertrude says to Hamlet (Act 3, Scene 4). If some measure of closure is within your reach, seize it. If closure is elusive, revisit the story you're telling, either to others or yourself.

Maybe it's time to change the narrative. That does not mean burying the truth. It means choosing how to interpret its role in the story of your life.

If you were given five minutes to provide a synopsis of your life so far, what would you say? You really ought to try this several different ways. For a high school reunion update. For a first date. For your grandchildren. For your own ears only.

There's the story we tell the world and the story we tell ourselves. We have many stories, but I think people should spend a bit more time examining what they sound like within their own heads. What we don't say becomes part of the way we express what we *do* say.

If you have experienced trauma, the initial experience was more than enough. Take care that you aren't re-traumatizing yourself by repressing the event and circumstances or by characterizing yourself forever as a powerless victim. That was who you were then, through no fault of your own. You get to choose the impact of the truth now.

The healing process may include embracing a cause or redressing a wrong. It may come through reconciliation or through a permanent break. Accept that you may never fully put the past to bed but do toss it a pillow. We shall all face our share of personal battles. That doesn't mean we should cultivate warfare as our personal truth.

You *do* have a choice. Don't wound yourself further by believing you don't.

Javier

Some relationships are mistakes worth making. This was another subject I did not cover with my students. I know, in fact, that some of my students believed it to be a tragedy that I would choose to be single. Their sympathy was touching but laughable.

In my life, I've received four marriage proposals. These were all honorable men—I just couldn't picture it. As my father likes to put it to strangers, "Victoria lives without contracts." I came close to saying "I do" only once.

I remember that since English was his second language, he wanted me to read to him something I found moving in my native tongue. I read to him a passage from Shakespeare where Juliet talks about Romeo being cut up into little stars after his death so that all the world would be in love with night and pay no heed to the garish sun. It made him cry. I remember thinking that this was part of what it meant to be Guatemalan.

He corrected me on my interpretation of "positive reinforce-ment." He as a nurse and I as a teacher. In the time that I knew him, he was a mechanic and then a nurse. When we woke in the morning, he would remind me that we both "got" to pursue our careers, as opposed to "had to."

He changed my thoughts on how I take my coffee. It used to be with a heavy pour of cream until he suggested that drinking coffee black honors the bean. I wasn't immediately convinced, but it struck me as a powerful argument. I haven't seen Javier for 20 years, but I still take my coffee black.

He was spontaneous and emotive, while I am measured and reserved. I was attracted immediately and unreservedly. We both had served in the military. We both wished to give more than we took. We had a song that we loved to dance to.

We had private jokes. Once, we were watching the news and there was a man pictured standing outside of a church. I've long forgotten the context. Javier sang softly, "I'm all alone" in a way that had us both laughing for no apparent reason. It became a thing, as things do. For months afterwards, one of us would find a reason to turn to the other and intone, "I'm all alone."

I called him from a field trip once. Nothing monumental had happened, but it occurred to me that he was the first person I thought of to call.

He had children from a previous relationship. I met them before I was comfortable doing so. I was upset with myself for not following my own instincts on the subject.

Turns out he was not committed to a monogamous re-lationship.

I started to depend on his attention, and that left me both

satisfied and unsettled. Perhaps not everyone is built for yearning, I thought.

It's funny what you learn about yourself when you are with someone else. Yet I'd do it all again, and I have no regrets about the way everything turned out. Whether for a time or forever, love is powerful.

Know When to Leave the Party

I love the English language for its power of expression and nuance. One can get lost in the swirl of semantics. When I left teaching, I technically *quit*. On paper, I *retired*. In my heart, it felt like abandonment. I had lost faith in those in charge of making timely and reasonable decisions. I doubted my own ability to adapt to a model of teaching so reliant upon technology.

There may come a day where you are faced with a similar decision. Ultimately, it comes down to what one feels is best for oneself. I didn't leave the building in a blaze of moral indignation, but I did make a definitive decision about the limits of my own flexibility and compromise. Turns out, I'm rather stubborn.

Many years ago, someone asked me when I would leave teaching. My answer was when it stopped being fun. It can be rewarding, heartbreaking, labor intensive, frustrating, and many other things. For me, it was all of those things. But it was always fun—until it wasn't. That may be a result of my own lack of imagination, adaptability, and tractability. And if so, then I definitely made the right decision. One should always know when to leave the party.

I struggled with what to call myself in the months after leaving the classroom. "Retired teacher" fills the space, but it felt like holding onto a label from my past. There are some roles that belong to us for life—others we have just for a time. So, who am I now? I'll be working on that one. It's time for me to learn the lesson that who we are is not determined by what we do.

Perhaps it's time to return to Uncle Michael's advice. *Everybody needs a project.*

BEING PRESENT TO RECEIVE

Just Breathe

I have an experiment for you. Take a light object, like a pen, and place it in front of you on the floor. From a standing position, reach down and pick up the object. As you do, be fully present and aware of the movements of your body. Okay, ready? Pick up the object.

Did you hold your breath during this activity? Chances are, you did. The reason? A part of you anticipated an action of some difficulty. Just imagine if you were about to move a couch. When we hold our breath, we make everything harder. We impose added resistance where it need not exist.

Test this theory when you need to open a jar. Have you ever struggled with this task? Do you recall the embarrassment of trying to force the lid off, only to hand the container to someone else who popped it off on the first attempt? Chances are, they weren't holding their breath.

When faced with a challenge, whether imposing or relatively minor, stop anticipating the worst. Seize the moment like a champ, with confidence, and while breathing normally. This technique operates on both a literal and metaphorical level. I love when that happens. The same holds true for contemplating changes yet to come.

Feelings of dread are so exhausting, and they can similarly be a kneejerk reaction to perceived difficulty. If you notice patterns of dread, you may have simply lapsed into a habit of anticipating hardship. Here's a simple test. If you hold a nine to five weekday job, how do you feel on a Sunday between midafternoon and early evening? Many people will report anxiety creeping in. Well, naturally you will not be able to sleep in, and there will be mental or physical exertion in your future. But ask yourself if your anxiety is commensurate with the task ahead. Once Monday morning is underway, you will undoubtedly feel calmer. Why? Because you are doing that which you had convinced yourself would be difficult.

While we're on the subject, if you find yourself carrying a tray of beverages, soup, condiments, etc., don't focus your gaze upon the items on the tray. If you do, you are far more likely to spill them. Look confidently in the direction you wish to travel. Trust in your intuition and in your own sense of balance.

Cafés and Other Sacred Places

Cafés are an oasis of creativity, civil discourse, and free Wi-Fi. There are recognized chains but consider giving the independently owned ones a try. They are great places to read, to write, and to people watch. As businesses began to reopen after the pandemic, I couldn't believe how much I had missed this simple pleasure. If I ever decide to pursue my van life fantasy, I look forward to discovering local haunts on the road.

On the home front, creating a nook can be similarly satisfying. A dedicated space for reflection can help to encourage introspection, innovation, and whimsy. A writing desk, a comfy chair, a prayer table, a picture window, or whatever else feels right. I live in a small loft apartment with two desks. One is actually a farm table that overlooks a bird-filled tree. The other overlooks the main street and gets direct sunlight. I can touch them both at the same time, but since I live in a tourist town, I can make conscious choices about whether it's a day to watch birds or people.

Carving out a space for personal reflection encourages thoughtfulness and mindfulness. It needn't cost anything, but it can be an investment in and reminder of the need to take it easy and to take stock of where we are and where we are going.

Nature as a Restorative

Whether you live in a rural, urban, or suburban setting, it's important to feel the sun on your face. The rain can be quite refreshing too. Find a way to get outside, whatever your situation. It's the best elixir I know for depressive symptoms, lack of clarity, and generalized dissatisfaction. I live on the Delaware River, so the towpath is a great walking option. I'm also lucky enough to live in a town with ample sidewalks. Yet, when the weather permits, hiking is my go-to form of exercise. For me, it's a form of meditation, where I can do some serious thinking or clear my mind entirely. Nature reminds you to breathe deeply, to notice simple beauty, and to be one with Mother Earth. Only you can take control of your vitamin D absorption.

Find a way to get your fill of this wonderful restorative. Get your family involved. Strive for 15 minutes a day. You don't have to walk. If you like gardening, you are truly blessed. Put your hands in the dirt and make things grow. If you like people watching, sit at the park. If you have a tennis ball, play fetch with your dog.

We are all part of nature, but it's easy to set ourselves apart as we become consumed with the demands of work, school, and chores. If you cannot free yourself from the routines because the obligation is too great, then add nature *to* the routine. It's an investment with enduring returns.

Traces of Places

They say the olfactory sense is closely tied to memory, and can reach the farthest back in time. I often associate smells with specific places. There is a certain scent to campfires in England. Once in a great while, someone will burn leaves in the States, and it rivals the scent, but it is never quite like it. In Louisiana, there is a progression of smells during the sugarcane season that is distinctive, ranging from molasses to dirty diaper. Near the mills, it is all-consuming and insistent. Manhattan is a curious pungent mix of street vendor pretzels and charcoal. The minute I set foot in the Port Authority, it greets me.

There's the smell of cut grass I always associate with my Aunt Sheila's lawn and the way her immaculate house carried the distinct scent of ammonia and a two-pack-a-day habit.

Those smells take us back in an instant, the way few other experiences can transport us. I tell you this so you are not taken by surprise when it happens. Often, we assume past associations and relationships are long buried and hence resolved. You may discover through the slightest whiff of a familiar scent—someone's cologne or perfume, a pipe, maybe a wet dog—that the memory is very much alive, whether comforting or confronting. I think that's what people really mean when they use the word "bittersweet."

The Mirror Confessions

If you fear public speaking, give this formidable task a try.

Look in the mirror and take note of what you see. To be clear, you're not looking for crow's feet. Not to get all esoteric and woo-woo, but you're trying to see the real you. Kudos if you can get through the exercise without laughing or blushing. Why is this activity painful for some, including me? Well, it's confronting, that's why. There is simply you, staring back without much to distract the sensitive viewer. If you're an introvert, the task may be even harder.

So why would we put ourselves through such a cringe-worthy task? To learn to gaze as lovingly at our own selves as we do at others. It takes practice.

The Ultimate Goal

Everything you want, you want for the same reason. To be happy. That's it. No more complicated than that. In other words, if you want a new car, it may be because you need a reliable vehicle, or you need room for more passengers, or you want to impress the neighbors. If you ask yourself why you want any of those things, and you follow the path long enough, the answer is always the same. Even if it is to impress others, sooner or later, you will track your motivation to your own worthiness, satisfaction, security, comfort, and happiness. That doesn't make you selfish—that makes you human.

So now that you know this, it's unnecessary to hold onto anything that makes you unhappy. If the new car is a gas guzzler, prohibitively expensive to insure, or makes you anxious when it comes to parking, it isn't what you bargained for. Solution? Get rid of it. No need to invest more time, money, or aggravation. Stop justifying the purchase, the move, or the decision. If it doesn't make you happy, it's no longer serving you.

What if something isn't making you happy, but it's non-negotiable, like an alimony payment? Then make your peace with it. That probably sounds insensitive and glib. But let's remember, the goal is happiness, and ultimately, it's in your hands.

The Universe
Is Always Listening

At 50, I broke my right wrist. I was climbing down from my sleeping loft, and the ladder slipped out from under me. It was a preventable accident caused by my negligence in not properly securing the ladder.

Such is life. You live, you learn. You screw up, you are humbled. Unfortunately, in the wake of two surgeries and a fair amount of hardware, the fingers of my right hand seemed to be permanently contracted. I initially worried that I might not be able to write properly or even type efficiently.

While recuperating at a friend's house, I got myself into a real funk. What if this injury would be an impediment to doing my job properly? What if through my own stupidity, I had just made my profession exponentially more difficult? What if I had to give up teaching?

As I sat convalescing in my friend's armchair, imagining worst-case scenarios, she asked if while she ran a few errands, I could let in the men who were coming to repair the house security system. When they arrived, even though it was the middle of winter, one of the men was in shorts, with a large tattoo of Hebrew writing visible on his leg. I asked him what it said. He flippantly replied that it was a matzo ball recipe and went on about his work.

I sat there wondering how I had offended this man. Now I was depressed *and* embarrassed. He soon returned and apologized for his curt tone. The question, he said, had caught him off guard, and he wished to explain. I told him he needn't, secretly hoping he would proceed, and he did. He told me that the tattoo was a biblical passage that gave him the strength to forge ahead in the aftermath of his wife's passing. He wanted to be strong for their son, and the tattoo was a reminder that life goes on. He welled up a bit as he explained, and by now, you know me and tears.

About this time, my friend returned to find two people weeping in her living room.

Once the man had left, I started thinking about the odds of a message from the universe reaching me while I sat in an armchair feeling sorry for myself. It had literally come to me by knocking on the door. From that day forward, I never worried about my right hand again. I figured if I were meant to keep teaching, I would. If it wasn't meant to be, then I would figure out how to do something else. Though my right hand would never quite be the same, over time it regained sufficient functionality.

In the meantime, I became left-handed with a surprising level of dexterity. I shall never forget that when I was feeling low, a stranger shared his personal story that allowed me to emerge from my own self-pity. I believe that meeting was meant to be.

Ignorance, Sometimes, Is Bliss

After I broke my wrist in the dead of night and my good friend Johnny drove me to the hospital, I met a young physician on call who suggested that it would be best if he pulled my arm into a more recognizable shape, as it was a veritable "s." He asked me to hold onto the rail of the gurney with the other hand. For some reason, this raised no red flags. I did as instructed and he pulled. I would later joke to my students that in this moment I saw God. "Allah, Mohammed, all the boys were there." For in that singular flash, I experienced such exquisite pain that I surely must have held the key to all the mysteries of the world. Sadly, I can recall none of them now.

Sometimes not knowing is better.

Do Something
Extraordinary

This was the final life lesson I gave to my students in June. It was an invitation to challenge themselves. Mind you, my students were already doing extraordinary things. Many were involved in mission work and with other volunteer organizations through their churches and local communities. I always stressed that this extraordinary thing didn't have to be wildly adventurous or philanthropic. It did need to be intentional and life-affirming.

I leave you with the same challenge. Become an example to others of what is possible in this exquisite journey.

Acknowledgments

I would like to thank Hannah Godshall, Nicole Gordienko, Rory Pruess, and Jan Illingworth for reading early versions of this book and giving invaluable feedback. Sandra Wendel and Lory Hough provided a framework for editing expectations. Many thanks to Jacqueline Parkison, my developmental editor from Reedsy. So many thanks to Julie Broad, Elissa Graeser, Dan England, Marc Lindsay, Lizzi Sandell, and the whole team at Book Launchers. To my favorite librarian, Lisa Maderic, for her advice about getting started. And special thanks to Andy Paul for his technical and emotional support.